COOKING AND B
DRIED F

Demonstrates the wide variety of
can be effectively and healthily incorporated
and special occasion cookery.

COOKING AND BAKING WITH DRIED FRUIT

by

RITA GREER

Illustrated by the author

THORSONS PUBLISHERS LIMITED
Wellingborough, Northamptonshire

First published 1984

British Library Cataloguing in Publication Data

Greer, Rita
  Cooking and baking with dried fruit.
  1. Cookery (Fruit, Dried)
  I. Title
  641.6'4   TX811

ISBN 0-7225-0884-0

Printed in Great Britain by
Richard Clay (The Chaucer Press) Ltd,
Bungay, Suffolk

CONTENTS

INTRODUCTION

Most of the recipes in this book are for everyday food — a much neglected area of cooking. The amounts of dried fruit vary from a little, merely as a garnish, to large quantities forming the main part of the ingredients. Dried fruit is a versatile as well as nourishing commodity. It can be used in savoury as well as sweet recipes, both raw and cooked. Colours vary from the pale cream of the peach to the deep amber of apricots, right through to the gingery gold of dates, the rich brown of figs and the bluish black of prunes. Some are sharp (apricots), others are sweet (sultanas/golden seedless raisins) and some extra sweet (dates). They are available all year round and keep well. With endless advantages like these there have had to be limits, otherwise the book could have run to several volumes. So, the recipes aim to be of the wholefood variety and vegetarian too. As well as these restraints I have added my own nutritional guidelines wherever possible — high-fibre, low-fat, sugar and salt, simple ingredients, etc. The recipes cover a wide field — soups, starters, salads, main meals, puddings, desserts, biscuits, scones and pastries, small cakes, buns, bars, cookies, cakes, fruit breads and yeasted buns, sauces, pickles, chutneys and jams, snacks, juices and sweets. The value of dried fruit in relation to special diets is also included. The selection is cosmopolitan with adapted recipes from all over the world and some new ones too.

People have used dried fruit for centuries. It reaches our kitchens from all over the world and in a time when the freezer seems to be king as the great preserver of food, dried fruit is still here to stay.

This book aims to broaden the horizons of any cook who wants to cook more often with dried fruit.

Nutrition Today

Like many people nowadays, I am appalled by the irresponsible attitude of so-called 'cookery experts' and writers regarding the subject of nutrition. (This is clearly shown in their high-fat, sugar and salt, low-fibre, added chemicals approach to their art.) Along with the food manufacturers and governments they must shoulder some of the blame for the effects of their policies on the health of the nations of the developed countries. Agricultural policies which produce surpluses in turn lead to bad eating habits, encouraged by producers, manufacturers and governments. Lack of education in the basic principles of nutrition is yet another factor in the alarming incidence of ill-health among us.

The medical profession is only just coming round to the idea that what we eat *may* be connected with the long term state of our health, but as a whole the profession doesn't really want to know. From time to time there is a feeble cry from some august medical body (which is encouraging) but it is soon drowned by the food manufacturers and advertisers.

Good health is beyond price. Poor eating habits can only undermine health. The present day leading 'food experts', apart from a few exceptions, are destined to go down in history as ludicrous puppets of the irresponsible organizations who do know better but won't pass on their knowledge for fear of a fall in profits. (The scandal of the NACNE report (UK) became a focus on the situation in 1983.)

But take heart, there is a definite movement away from the poor values of the last three or four decades. People are becoming more informed about nutrition, the average person does value good health and genuine health is becoming commercially successful. Let's hope that one day it will be more successful than the junk food trade and then we'll all have the chance to eat in a healthy way without being pressured in the opposite direction.

Meanwhile you can take matters into your own hands, in your own kitchen. Your reward should be good health for yourself and your family.

Nutrition

We tend to think that progress has led only to improvement in the way people are nourished. Unfortunately this is not always the case. Bread is just one example where the staple loaf has degenerated into a chemical kind of cake that makes nutritional nonsense. (Our grandparents and great-grandparents actually ate much better bread than the majority of us. It was made from stoneground wheat, organically grown and baked without chemical improvers or preservatives and too much salt.)

You can avoid this basic nutritional hazard by baking your own bread at home using a good quality wholemeal, stoneground flour. Make it with fresh yeast and with the bare minimum salt. Eat several slices a day instead of filling junk foods.

Sugar

There is very little to be gained by using raw cane sugar in the same amounts as you were using white. Sugar is sugar, whatever the colour and most of us eat far too much of it. Avoid sugary foods and save on the dental bills!

Salt

The majority of the population eats far too much salt. Much of it is contained in junk, convenience foods, bread and breakfast cereals. Being a cheap preservative the manufacturers of foods really don't care how much of it they use. Combine this bad eating habit with the avoidance of fresh vegetables and you have the classic too-little-potassium-and-too-much-salt syndrome that can be a ticket to a heart attack, stroke or some other circulatory disease.

Fat

When fat is around in various surpluses we are encouraged to eat too much of it from all sides. Cut right down on hard cheeses, high-fat milk and food which contains a lot of fat, for example, peanuts, nut butters, butter, margarine and cream. Grill foods in preference to frying. The fact that you fry in unsaturated fat and use it instead of butter, in the form of margarine, isn't going to improve matters if you still persist in eating too much.

Fibre

Fibre is nature's packaging material. Except for a few voices crying in the wilderness for decades, fibre has not been considered to be of much importance. How wrong the experts have been! Use stoneground, wholemeal flour for bread, cooking and baking. Eat plenty of fresh vegetables, eat one kind of pulse everyday (beans, peas, lentils) and this should give all the fibre you need. (Unless there is a medical reason there is no need to take extra bran.)

Vegetarian Food

There are two popular myths about vegetarian food. One is that it is positively dangerous and the other is that it will cure all ills. Neither of these two ideas make sense. On a vegetarian diet it is still possible to eat unwisely by making the same mistakes in the balance of the diet as the meat/fish eaters. Too little fibre, far too much dairy fat, too much sugar and salt, too little vegetables and fibre.

Diet Balance for Vegetarians

About half the food eaten should be in the form of vegetables and fruit. About a third should be wholegrains and pulses and the remaining one sixth can be fats from dairy produce, nuts, oil and fat spreads (both saturated and unsaturated). The protein element is distributed in wholemeal bread, dairy products (milk, cheese, eggs) and a small amount in vegetables (such as potatoes), pulses and wholegrains. A diet with plenty of variety should provide you with the combinations of foods that will offer maximum nutritional value. Eating as many fresh foods as possible instead of processed ones is another plus.

Vitamin Deficiency

A medical note here about being a strict vegetarian. If you do not eat meat or fish you should really top up with vitamin B_{12}. (Most people on an ordinary diet will get their supply from meats.) You cannot obtain this vitamin in large enough amounts from vegetarian foods, and your body needs it for nerve function and to prevent anaemia.

1.

BUYING AND USING DRIED FRUIT

There are basically three kinds of dried fruit — those from the vine (currants, sultanas/golden seedless raisins and raisins), those from trees (figs, dates, apples, pears, nectarines, apricots, peaches and bananas) and pineapple and papaya from plants. They are all suitable for drying, i.e. most of their moisture can be evaporated. In this way their natural fruit sugars can preserve them.

Dried fruits contain a selection of vitamins, minerals, fruit sugar, a little protein, sometimes a little fat and always fibre. By drying the fruits some of their original nutrients are lost but others are concentrated. Each kind of fruit has its own personality — flavour, colour and appearance. Some need a little extra help with their preservation but most are simply dried in the sun.

Those fruits which cannot merely be sun-dried are liable to spoil by growing moulds. Sulphur dioxide is used in very small amounts to prevent this where necessary. (This can be removed by soaking in water and/or cooking.) Potassium sorbate (sorbic acid), a polyunsaturated fatty acid, is another preservative used to stop yeasts forming. This is quite harmless. Mineral oil is sometimes used to keep fruits separate instead of in sticky lumps. Always look on the packet at the list of ingredients when you purchase dried fruit to see just what you are buying.

People have been using dried fruits for centuries. This is not surprising as they are an excellent addition to the diet, not just nutritionally but also because they add variety and are available all year round. They keep well and are relatively inexpensive. Here are a few details about them:

Raisins
Raisins are made from white grapes, from both grapes which have seeds and those which are seedless. The varieties which have seeds are usually de-seeded before they are packed and are thought generally to have a better flavour than the seedless varieties. Best buys for de-seeded raisins are the orange or dark brown varieties. The fruit should be flat and sticky. Best seedless raisins are the dark brown ones from the USA but any golden, slightly plump raisins will be a good buy. Muscatels are large, expensive raisins for eating raw. Most of these will have seeds in them. Nutritional value: calcium, iron (in seedless varieties), phosphorus, potassium and Vitamin B_1.

Sultanas (Golden seedless raisins)
Sultanas (golden seedless raisins) are made from white seedless grapes. Look for plump, golden fruit. Nutritional value: calcium, potassium and vitamins B_2 and B_6.

Currants
Currants are made from black seedless grapes. Best buy is black, fleshy-looking, medium-sized fruit. Avoid reddish coloured ones and the very small varieties. Nutritional value: high calcium level, iron, potassium, Vitamins A, B_1 and B_3.

All three vine fruits contain a little protein, copper, iron, calcium, magnesium, phosphorus, sodium, potassium and Vitamins A, B_1, B_2 and B_3. Seedless raisins and sultanas (golden seedless raisins) also contain Vitamin B_6.

Dried Apricots
Dried apricots are available in de-stoned halves or as whole pitted fruits. Slab apricots are pieces of the stoned fruit packed tightly. Use these for pie fillings and purées, jams and chutneys. The dried apricot is the king of dried fruit regarding nutritional value. It has high concentrations of Vitamin A, iron, potassium, phosphorus and

calcium. It is also the most attractively coloured fruit — pale to deep amber.

Dried Apples
Dried apples are the good mixers of the dried fruit family. They combine well with any other dried fruit. Nutritionally speaking, they are the poor cousins as they lack Vitamin A and have substantially lower levels of nutrients.

Dried Peaches
Dried peaches have a delicate cream or creamy-pinkish colour. Nutritional value: very high level of potassium and phosphorus, B_3 and even a little Vitamin C. Usually sold as pitted halves. When soaked they swell to quite large half fruits.

Dried Pears
The most subtle tasting of all the dried fruits, they contain about double the fibre of the apricots, apple and peaches. Usually sold as pitted halves.

Dried Nectarines
Nectarines are similar to peaches regarding nutritional qualities but with a much stronger flavour and colour. Not yet widely available as the crop is small and specialized.

All these tree fruits (apricots, apples, peaches, pears and nectarines) contain a little protein, calcium, iron, magnesium, phosphorus, sodium and potassium, Vitamins A (except apples), B_1, B_2, B_3 and a little Vitamin C.

Prunes
Special varieties of plums are dried to make prunes. The best quality ones are usually left whole and the cheapest ones are sold as prune pieces or even purée. A special quality of 'tenderized prune' is now available. These need only 7 or 8 minutes cooking and no soaking. Pitted prunes can also be bought and these have their stones removed before drying. Nutritional value: high potassium and Vitamin A, good levels of iron.

Figs

The fig is the demon king of dried fruits probably due to its well-known laxative properties. Nutritional value: very high potassium, high fibre, calcium, iron, magnesium and phosphorus. It is quite natural for figs to go 'sugary' as their natural sugars crystallize. Some will be sprayed with a fine coating of glucose syrup. (This can be washed off.) There are three types of figs on sale. Layer figs are fan-shaped and pressed flat. Sometimes these are pieces and not whole figs. Pulled figs are sold in a slab and although they look a bit of a jumble in fact whole figs are used and not pieces. Lerida figs are squashed completely flat into circles. (I have bought these before threaded on string like discs.)

Dates

Dates come to us from the arid deserts of the world. (If there is one thing a date palm hates it is water above ground of any kind.) The best eating dates are Deglet Nour — a beautiful golden orange colour. Buy dark brown slab dates for cooking as they are much cheaper and already pitted. Avoid dates or chopped dates rolled in sugar as the dates themselves are incredibly sweet. Adding more sugar is a nonsense. Nutritional value: potassium and calcium.

Bananas

Dried bananas are not available all year round because they are only produced when there is a surplus of fresh bananas. They are dark greyish or orangey brown in colour, very hard and fibrous looking. They are sold as chopped (small) pieces or in oblongs, and are mainly used as a substitute for sweets and confectionery. (At the time of writing I regret there is no available, reliable information on the nutritional value of dried bananas.)

Prunes, figs and dates all contain calcium, iron, copper (except prunes), magnesium, phosphorus, sodium and potassium, Vitamins A, B_1, B_2, B_3, and B_6. Prunes contain a little Vitamin C.

Buying and storing of dried fruit

You will find the best quality fruits at good grocers and health food stores. While preparing this book I tried all kinds of available brands. While some brands were of such poor quality as to be practically unusable, the most consistent for high quality was one particular brand. After a few culinary disasters I stuck to this brand and had good results every time.

Although dried fruits keep well if stored in containers, in a cool dry place, don't keep them too long on your shelves before using. Buy small amounts and use within a couple of months. Dried fruits are always available, with the exception of nectarines and bananas, all year round.

While some writer-cooks seem to work via the typewriter only, I do feel obliged to cook and bake every recipe in my books, often several times, to get them right. This not only calls for a lot of energy, fortitude (especially with the washing up) and a full housekeeping purse, but a mountain of ingredients as well. I am grateful to Petty Wood Ltd (whose *Epicure* brand of dried fruits I prefer) for samples of their products with which to experiment. They are a pleasure to cook with.

Further Reading about Dried Fruit
You really could do no better than to read *Dried Fruit* by Robert Dark (Thorsons). It gives fascinating information about the growing and processing of dried fruits and their countries of origin as well as facts about nutritional aspects. Written by someone who has worked in the dried fruit trade for years this is a very useful and authoritative little book.

Notes on Using Yeast
As fresh yeast is now widely available I have given instructions for using this in the recipes. However, if you wish to use dried yeast, please use *half* the quantities given in the recipes for fresh yeast. Buy a kind that is not sold in a transparent packet. Dried active yeast has a short life and if it kept in the dark it has a better chance of getting to you in a still active state.

One of the last bastions of good bread has been the home-made variety, freshly baked with simple ingredients. Now the food manufacturers are infiltrating our home kitchens. A range of extraordinary chemical combinations posing as yeast and 'improvers' has arrived in the shops. If used at home they will put your own bread in the same category as the junk bread made and sold commercially. For best results use plain, simple ingredients.

If you are lucky and can buy one of the new 'instant' yeasts, please do, for they make cooking so much quicker. This type of yeast is mixed in dry with the flour and does not need to be creamed or left to work in warm water and sugar like dried yeast. However, it is this very kind of yeast that is now being assaulted by the food scientists. Look carefully on the packet to see exactly what the ingredients are. If the list is long, avoid.

A Note on Flour
Here too is an area that has begun to interest the food manufacturer and it is now possible to buy really poor quality 'brown' flour in most supermarkets. You may be lucky and have a mill in your area which produces stoneground flour, locally grown. In UK 'brown flour' can mean white flour dyed brown. 'Wheatmeal' is also another camouflage word. Buy 'wholemeal' or 'wholewheat' stoneground. This will be just what it says — the whole wheat (including fibre) ground between stones. So, don't be conned into buying flour which isn't all it seems.

Self-Raising Flour
This is not mentioned in the book other than here. I have given plain wholemeal flour plus baking powder because not everyone can obtain wholemeal self-raising flour. However, if it is easily obtained, and you would prefer to use it rather than making your own, just do a straight substitute for the wholemeal flour in all the recipes that call for flour plus a baking powder. The only ones where you will need a little extra lift are the scones and muffins, so for these add extra baking powder to your self-raising flour.

Steaming
This is a slow method of cooking on the top of the stove. The dish is prepared and put into a basin, covered with a greaseproof paper lid and put into a saucepan of boiling water. This is kept simmering for hours if need be.

General advice:

1. The lid should be a double layer of greaseproof paper, tied on with a suitable kind of string, i.e. one which will withstand the steam. A handle of string is also required. For puddings which will rise during cooking a pleat should be made in the greaseproof lid to accommodate the extra.
2. The pudding basin should be of a kind that will withstand the heat. (Certain types of plastic ones will just melt.) Heatproof glass or china ones are ideal.
3. The basin should be kept from direct contact with the bottom of the saucepan. Use either a metal grid or 3 metal forks or spoons.
4. The water level in the saucepan should not be allowed to fall below two thirds of the way up the basin. This means you will need to top up the water level from time to time. Use boiling water to do this, not cold, to maintain the temperature.
5. The boiling saucepan should have a lid on during the steaming. This should not be clamped on tightly but should leave a small gap for the steam to escape.
6. The water in the saucepan should not be allowed to get into the basin.

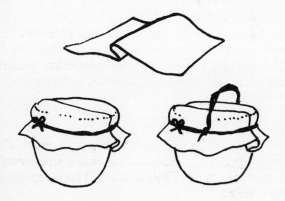

Preparing Dried Fruit for Use in Cooking and Baking

Bearing in mind the lack of cleanliness in the countries of origin, the long distances it has to travel and the number of hands it passes through before ending up in our kitchens it is no surprise to learn that *all dried fruit should be washed thoroughly just before use*. Even if it says 'washed' on the packet, still put it under the cold tap, in a colander or sieve and wash it well. This will help to remove preservatives as well as general dirt. Vine fruits can be picked over to remove stalks and any other foreign bodies such as the odd leaf.

Dried fruit that is to go into cakes, breads and buns e.g. the smaller types of fruit, does not need to be soaked, unless indicated in a recipe. Other kinds such as apricots, fruit salad, prunes, pears, peaches, etc, need to be soaked to reconstitute them. They will absorb quite a lot of water, slowly, over several hours, so this is best done overnight. Unless the recipes direct to the contrary, soak for about 12 hours, after washing. Cover with cold water in a basin large enough to allow for their swelling to two or three times their original size.

After soaking, the fruit is usually cooked in water, in a saucepan, for about 20 to 30 minutes to tenderize the fruit. If there is any stoning to be done this is the best time to do it, when the fruit is soft again.

Sticky fruits that need to be chopped can be cut with a sharp knife, lightly greased with cooking oil, or a dusting of flour.

2.

SOUPS, STARTERS AND MAIN MEALS

Dried fruits, in spite of their sweetness, can make a marvellous addition to curried dishes, and those which contain cheese, herbs and spices or other fruits.

APPLE SOUP
Serves 4

The perfect soup to serve in a heatwave. Makes a cool and refreshing start to a meal.

Imperial (Metric)
1 lb (455g) cooking apples
1 pint (570ml) water
Finely grated rind of 1 lemon
Juice of 1 lemon
1 red pepper, de-seeded and
    chopped
3 oz (85g) raisins
2 teaspoonsful arrowroot mixed into
    3 tablespoonsful cold water
2 oz (55g) raw cane sugar
Chopped parsley for garnish

American
1 pound cooking apples
2½ cupsful water
Finely grated rind of 1 lemon
Juice of 1 lemon
1 red pepper, de-seeded and
    chopped
½ cupful raisins
2 teaspoonsful arrowroot mixed into
    3 tablespoonsful cold water
⅓ cupful raw cane sugar
Chopped parsley for garnish

Continued overleaf.

1. Peel and core the apples. Slice into a saucepan.

2. Pour in the water, lemon rind and juice.

3. Add the chopped pepper and the raisins.

4. Bring to the boil and simmer until soft.

5. Stir the arrowroot mixture into the soup and add the sugar. Bring to the boil and simmer while you stir, for 3 minutes.

6. Allow to cool and then liquidize to a smooth purée (paste). Chill in the fridge.

7. Serve chilled with a sprinkle of chopped parsley.

CHEESE AND RAISIN SOUP
Serves 3 or 4

A very filling soup. Serve with fingers of dry, thin, wholemeal toast and follow with a low fat main course and sweet.

Imperial (Metric)	American
1 small onion, peeled and sliced thinly	1 small onion, peeled and sliced thinly
2 teaspoonsful sunflower oil	2 teaspoonsful sunflower oil
1 heaped teaspoonful wholemeal flour	1 heaped teaspoonful wholewheat flour
½ pint (285ml) cold water	1⅓ cupful cold water
½ pint (285ml) skimmed milk	1⅓ cupful skimmed milk
2 teaspoonsful soya sauce	2 teaspoonsful soy sauce
1 tablespoonful raisins	1 tablespoonful raisins
Freshly ground black pepper	Freshly ground black pepper
3 oz (85g) finely grated Cheddar cheese	⅔ cupful finely grated Cheddar cheese
1 tablespoonful chopped parsley (fresh)	1 tablespoonful chopped parsley (fresh)

1. Fry the onion in the oil until transparent, using a saucepan.

2. Blend the flour in a cup with 2 tablespoonsful of the water. Stir into the rest of the cold water and pour into the onion mixture. Stir well.

3. Add the skimmed milk, soya sauce and raisins. Bring to the boil and simmer for 3 minutes, while you stir. Season to taste with the pepper.

4. Continue simmering (don't boil) and sprinkle in the cheese. Stir until it has all melted.

5. Sprinkle in the parsley and serve hot, at once.

Note: If you let this soup boil after adding the cheese, it will separate out and the soup will be spoiled.

MUSHROOMS À LA GRECQUE

Serves 3 as a starter

Imperial (Metric)	American
¼ pint (140ml) red wine	⅔ cupful red wine
½ pint (285ml) water	1⅓ cupsful water
1 oz (30g) raisins	1 heaped tablespoonful raisins
1 shallot, sliced thinly	1 shallot, sliced thinly
3 tinned tomatoes, chopped small	3 canned tomatoes, chopped small
1 heaped teaspoonful tomato purée	1 heaped teaspoonful tomato paste
2 tablespoonsful sunflower oil	2 tablespoonsful sunflower oil
2 teaspoonsful raw cane sugar	2 teaspoonsful raw cane sugar
5 coriander seeds	5 coriander seeds
8 peppercorns (whole)	8 peppercorns (whole)
2 pinches dried thyme	2 pinches dried thyme
½ lb (225g) button mushrooms	½ pound button mushrooms
Freshly ground black pepper (optional)	Freshly ground black pepper (optional)
Chopped, fresh parsley for garnish	Chopped, fresh parsley for garnish

1. Put all the ingredients except the mushrooms into a saucepan and bring to the boil. Simmer for about 5 minutes.

2. Wash the mushrooms and stir into the pan with the liquid. Bring back to the boil and simmer for about 10 minutes.

3. Remove the mushrooms with a perforated spoon (this will partly drain them) and put into 3 serving dishes.

4. Boil the liquid to reduce it. Pour over the mushrooms and leave to get cold. Sprinkle with freshly ground black pepper if you think necessary.

5. Serve chilled from the fridge and turn the mushrooms over in the sauce before serving. Sprinkle with a little freshly chopped parsley and serve with wholemeal toast.

Note: If you don't have a shallot use 2 spring onions (scallions), finely chopped.

CURRIED EGG SCRAMBLE
Make scrambled egg in the usual way but with a sprinkle of sultanas (golden seedless raisins) and mild curry powder to taste. Serve on hot wholemeal toast. Makes a good starter or snack.

SWEET CARROTS
Cook carrots in the usual way and toss in the minimum amount of butter. Serve hot, sprinkled with ½ a chopped, stoned date per portion and a sprinkle of chopped parsley.

TIPSY GARNISH
Soak raisins in a little sherry until plump. Add to a little heated butter and use as a garnish for calabrese or broccoli.

MULLIGATAWNY SOUP
Flavour any vegetable soup to taste with mild curry powder and a few pinches of garam masala. Add a sprinkle of raisins or sultanas (golden seedless raisins).

CURRIED BEANS
Soak a few sultanas (golden seedless raisins) or raisins in hot water for a few minutes. Add to baked beans in tomato sauce (highly popular UK delicacy!) and add mild curry powder to taste. Serve on wholemeal toast.

Main Meals

BAKED ONIONS

Imperial (Metric)	American
2 large Spanish onions	2 large Spanish onions
1 slice wholemeal bread made into crumbs	1 slice wholewheat bread made into crumbs
2 oz (55g) grated Cheddar cheese	½ cupful grated Cheddar cheese
2 heaped teaspoonsful grated apple	2 heaped teaspoonsful grated apple
1 level teaspoonful sultanas	1 slightly heaped teaspoonful golden seedless raisins
2 pinches dried ginger	2 pinches dried ginger
1 teaspoonful cider vinegar	1 teaspoonful cider vinegar
1 egg, beaten	1 egg, beaten
Freshly ground black pepper to taste	Freshly ground black pepper to taste

1. Peel the onions and part-cook in boiling water for about 15 minutes. Drain and cool.

2. Preheat oven at 350°F/180°C (Gas Mark 4).

3. Carefully, with a teaspoon, take out the centres of the onions, so that you leave a cavity.

4. Chop the onion centres and mix with the remaining ingredients.

5. Fill the onion cavities with the stuffing and bake above centre of the oven for about 50 minutes.

6. Serve hot as a main course with green vegetables and potatoes.

BEAN AND VEGETABLE CURRY
Serves 3 or 4

Imperial (Metric)	American
2 teaspoonsful vegetable oil	2 teaspoonsful vegetable oil
1 onion, peeled and sliced	1 onion, peeled and sliced
2 heaped teaspoonsful mild curry powder	2 heaped teaspoonsful mild curry powder

1 heaped teaspoonful coriander
½ cooking apple, chopped
1 tablespoonful raisins
3 teaspoonsful soya sauce
1 carrot, sliced
1 small turnip, peeled and sliced
½ red or green pepper, de-seeded and chopped
2 oz (55g) mushrooms, sliced
4 prunes
1 medium tin (plain) beans
1 tablespoonful wholemeal flour mixed with 3 tablespoonsful water
2 teaspoonsful garam masala

1 heaped teaspoonful coriander
½ cooking apple, chopped
1 tablespoonful raisins
2 heaped teaspoonsful mild curry powder
3 teaspoonsful soy sauce
1 carrot, sliced
1 small turnip, peeled and sliced
½ red or green pepper, de-seeded and chopped
2 medium-sized mushrooms, sliced
4 prunes
1 can (plain) beans
1 tablespoonful wholewheat flour mixed with 3 tablespoonsful water
2 teaspoonsful garam masala

1. Put the oil into a saucepan and fry the onion until transparent with the curry powder and ground coriander.

2. Add the apple, raisins, soya sauce, vegetables, prunes and beans. Put in enough water to cover and bring to the boil. Simmer for 20 minutes with the lid on.

3. Add the flour and water thickening and the garam masala. Bring back to the boil and cook for 3 minutes while you stir.

4. Serve hot with plain boiled rice, chapatis, chutney, and a dish of sliced tomatoes sprinkled with chopped walnuts (English walnuts) as a garnish.

Note: Any kind of cooked beans will do, for example, haricot or kidney beans. As such a small amount is required tinned, ready cooked ones are a good idea. However, if you wish, soak and cook your own to add to the curry.

CURRIED EGGS
Serves 4

Imperial (Metric)	American
8 small eggs	8 small eggs
2 onions, chopped and sliced	2 onions, chopped and sliced
1 tablespoonful vegetable oil	1 tablespoonful vegetable oil
Small piece root ginger, peeled	Small piece root ginger, peeled
2 heaped teaspoonsful mild curry powder	2 heaped teaspoonsful mild curry powder
2 cloves garlic, peeled	2 cloves garlic, peeled
3 tomatoes, chopped	3 tomatoes, chopped
1 tablespoonful soya sauce	1 tablespoonful soy sauce
4 oz (115g) fresh or frozen peas	1 cupful fresh or frozen peas
1 heaped tablespoonful sultanas	1 heaped tablespoonful golden seedless raisins
1 tablespoonful wholemeal flour mixed with 2 teaspoonsful water	1 tablespoonful wholewheat flour mixed with 2 tablespoonsful water
½ tablespoonful garam masala	½ tablespoonful garam masala

1. Boil the eggs, starting with cold water. Bring to the boil and cook for 7 minutes then plunge into cold water.

2. Use a large saucepan to fry the onion in the oil until transparent.

3. Add the root ginger, chopped finely, the curry powder and the garlic put through a garlic crusher. Stir-fry for another minute.

4. Put in the tomatoes, soy sauce and peas. Top up with water to cover and bring to the boil. Simmer while you stir, until the peas are tender. Add the sultanas (golden seedless raisins).

5. Shell the eggs and wash under the cold tap to make sure no little pieces of shell remain.

6. Pour in the flour and water thickening, add the garam masala and bring to the boil again. Stir and cook for 3 minutes then add the eggs.

7. Cook for another 5 minutes, being careful not to spoil the eggs.

8. Serve with plain boiled brown rice, chapatis, chutney and plates of thinly sliced cucumber and watercress sprigs.

Note: More mild curry powder can be added to taste.

CURRIED OMELETTE
Serves 2

Imperial (Metric)	American
1 tablespoonful vegetable oil	1 tablespoonful vegetable oil
1 small onion, finely chopped	1 small onion, finely chopped
2 boiled potatoes, diced	2 boiled potatoes, diced
1 portion diced, cooked vegetables	1 portion diced, cooked vegetables
1 tomato, sliced	1 tomato, sliced
1 tablespoonful sultanas	1 tablespoonful golden seedless raisins
2 eggs	2 eggs
½ teaspoonful mild curry powder	½ teaspoonful mild curry powder

1. Fry the onion in the oil until transparent, using a heavy-based frying pan (skillet).

2. Add the remaining cooked vegetables and stir-fry to heat through.

3. Add the tomato slices and sprinkle in the sultanas (golden seedless raisins).

4. Beat the eggs with the curry powder.

5. Pour over the mixture in the pan and cook for about 3 minutes until the bottom has set.

6. Put under a medium grill to cook the top.

7. Cut in half and serve with a green salad and a little plain boiled brown rice (optional).

CHEESE AND RAISIN QUICHE

A sweet and sour quiche to serve for lunch or dinner (6 servings) with salad. This can also be used as a party snack (10 servings) or for picnics.

Base:

Imperial (Metric)	American
Wholemeal pastry to line a 7 in. (18cm) dish (page 74)	Wholewheat pastry to line a 7 inch dish (page 74)

Filling:

Imperial (Metric)	American
2 eggs	2 eggs
½ pint (225g) milk	1⅓ cupsful milk
3 oz (85g) grated Cheddar cheese	⅔ cupful grated Cheddar cheese
1 heaped tablespoonful raisins	1 heaped tablespoonful raisins

1. Preheat oven at 450°F/230°C (Gas Mark 8). You will need the top shelf and a baking sheet to put the quiche dish on.

2. Roll out the pastry and line the quiche dish. Prick all over with a fork. Trim off the pastry neatly round the edge and very carefully, press the edge slightly over the rim of the dish. (This is to stop it collapsing on to the base.)

3. Put into the preheated oven, on the top shelf and on the baking sheet. This will ensure even cooking for the base.

4. Bake for 15 minutes, then lower the heat to 375°F/190°C (Gas Mark 5). Take the pastry case out of the oven.

5. To make the filling, whisk the eggs with the milk, then stir in the cheese.

6. Pour into the partly baked pastry case and sprinkle in the raisins.

7. Put carefully back into the oven on the lower heat and on the centre shelf for 30 minutes to finish cooking.

8. Serve hot from the oven, or cold. Either way this quiche can be
    served with salad.

If serving as part of a meal make sure the remaining courses are very
low in fat. If you would like this quiche to be even lower in fat (bearing
in mind there is margarine in the pastry and fat in the egg yolks, milk
and cheese) use dried skimmed milk which is very low in fat. You
will need to make up the milk with double the quantity of powder
given on the instructions or the quiche will not set.

(I never cease to be appalled at what glamour cooks can do to quiche
to make it as high in fat as possible — cream, extra egg yolks and
mountains of cheese. Wonderful entertainment for the palate but
nutritionally a disaster!)

PIZZA

Serve hot with the topping still sizzling, as a meal in itself with a side salad or in smaller portions (serves 8) as a hearty and tasty starter.

Scone base:

Imperial (Metric)
½ lb (225g) wholemeal flour
2 teaspoonsful baking powder
2 oz (55g) polyunsaturated margarine
⅓ pint (200ml) cold milk

American
2 cupsful wholewheat flour
2 teaspoonsful baking powder
5 tablespoonsful polyunsaturated margarine
¾ cupful cold milk

1. Mix flour and baking powder in a bowl. Rub in the margarine. Add the milk and mix to a stiff dough. Roll out using more flour. Shape into a round and place on a greased baking sheet ready for the topping sauce and other toppings.

2. Put on the toppings of your choice and bake above centre of oven, preheated at 425°F/220°C (Gas Mark 7) for about 25 minutes.

3. Serve hot, cut into wedges.

Sauce I plus Topping:

Imperial (Metric)
1 tablespoonful vegetable oil
2 onions, peeled and sliced
1 or 2 cloves garlic, peeled
1 tablespoonful fresh parsley, chopped
4 pinches dried basil
Freshly ground black pepper
Green or red peppers, chopped
Mushrooms, sliced
Courgette, sliced (optional)
4 oz (115g) Cheddar cheese, grated
Raisins

American
1 tablespoonful vegetable oil
2 onions, peeled and sliced
1 or 2 cloves garlic, peeled
1 tablespoonful fresh parsley, chopped
4 pinches dried basil
Freshly ground black pepper
Green or red peppers, chopped
Mushrooms, sliced
Zucchini, sliced (optional)
1 cupful Cheddar cheese, grated
Raisins

1. Fry the onions in the oil until transparent. Crush in the garlic. Add herbs and season with pepper to taste. Spread over the pizza base.

2. Sprinkle with chopped green or red peppers, sliced mushrooms, sliced courgette (zucchini).

3. Finish off with a layer of grated Cheddar cheese and a sprinkle of raisins.

4. Bake and serve.

Sauce II plus Topping:

Imperial (Metric)	**American**
1 medium tin of peeled tomatoes	1 medium can of peeled tomatoes
4 pinches dried or fresh oregano	4 pinches dried or fresh oregano
1 clove of garlic, peeled and crushed	1 clove of garlic, peeled and crushed
Sprinkle of raw cane sugar to taste	Sprinkle of raw cane sugar to taste.
Mushrooms, sliced, *or* mixture of cooked vegetables, i.e. sweetcorn, red and green peppers, peas	Mushrooms, sliced, *or* mixture of cooked vegetables, i.e. sweetcorn, red and green peppers, peas
4 oz (115g) Cheddar cheese, grated	1 cupful Cheddar cheese, grated
Date pieces	Date pieces

1. Mash the tomatoes and mix with the oregano, garlic and sugar. Season to taste with freshly ground black pepper and spread over the pizza base.

2. Top with either sliced mushrooms or a mixture of cooked vegetables — such as sweetcorn, red and green peppers, peas, etc.

3. Finish off with a layer of grated Cheddar cheese and a sprinkle of chopped, stoned date pieces.

4. Bake and serve hot cut into wedges.

Note: There are no hard and fast rules for pizza, except that it should be crisp on the outside and soft in the middle, with the base risen and a moist topping. The dried fruit in this recipe acts as a substitute for black olives. If you have made up the Pickled Prunes recipe (page 176), these are excellent, cut into olive-sized pieces. Try to arrange the dried fruit in a pattern as it sets off the pale golden colour of the cheese and looks best arranged neatly.

If you are really in a hurry and don't have time to make either of the sauces, brush the top of the scone base with vegetable oil and put on a layer of sliced, fresh tomatoes. Season with black pepper and cover with a layer of grated Cheddar cheese. Dot with raisins or chopped stoned prunes and bake. A clove of garlic can be crushed over the tomatoes with a sprinkle of raw cane sugar to taste.

If you are baking bread and would prefer a bread-based pizza then reserve some of the dough. Roll out on a floured worktop and place on a greased baking sheet. Put on the sauce and topping of your choice and let the pizza rise for about 15 minutes, in a warm place, before baking. This type of pizza should only require 15 to 20 minutes on the top shelf. Use the same oven setting as for the 'Scone Base' type pizza.

SAVOURY RICE
Serves 3 or 4

Imperial (Metric)	American
4 oz (115g) brown rice	½ cupful brown rice
1 medium onion, peeled and chopped	1 medium onion, peeled and chopped
1 tablespoonful sunflower oil	1 tablespoonful sunflower oil
4 oz (115g) chopped mushrooms	1½ cupsful chopped mushrooms
3 teaspoonsful soya sauce	3 teaspoonsful soy sauce
1 small red pepper, de-seeded and chopped	1 small red pepper, de-seeded and chopped
4 oz (115g) cooked peas	⅔ cupful cooked peas
1 tablespoonful raisins	1 tablespoonful raisins
1 heaped tablespoonful chopped walnuts	1 heaped tablespoonful chopped English walnuts
Freshly ground black pepper	Freshly ground black pepper
parsley for garnish	Parsley for garnish

1. Bring a large pan of water to the boil. Put in the rice and bring
    back to the boil. Stir just once and then simmer for about 30
    minutes, or until the rice is tender but still firm. While the rice
    is cooking prepare the remaining ingredients.

2. Fry the onion in the oil until transparent, using a saucepan.

3. Add the mushrooms, soya sauce, red pepper, peas and raisins.
    Put in enough water to prevent them sticking and stir-fry for
    5 minutes.

4. Stir in the nuts and cooked rice and season to taste with black
    pepper.

5. Serve hot, garnished with parsley. Grilled tomatoes make a good
    accompaniment.

Note: Can be served in small portions as a starter, or, as a main dish.
Follow with a high protein pudding or sweet, i.e. one with milk or
cheese as a main ingredient.

3.

SALADS

Salads With Dried Fruit

Before giving you salad ideas, here are some thoughts on dressings to accompany them. Moistening salads with dressing makes them easy to eat. Some salads, already moist, will need very little dressing. If your salads leave a puddle of dressing at the bottom of the bowl then it means you are using too much. As it is difficult to assess how much is too much until it is too late, here is my personal cure for this bad habit. Make the salad and remove half from the bowl. Dress what is in the bowl and then add the other half of the salad. Turn over with two spoons to distribute evenly. A very, very light coating is all that is needed. (Generous use of thick dressings which completely coat the salad with a sauce effect are a commercial idea to make you use — and buy more — than you need!)

Here are three kinds of dressing to use with the salad ideas that follow:

FRENCH DRESSING

This is probably the most widely used thin dressing and will suit any kind of salad.

1 teaspoonful made French mustard
1 tablespoonful wine or cider vinegar
3 tablespoonsful sunflower oil
Freshly ground black pepper

1. Put all the ingredients into a screwtop jar. Replace the lid and shake vigorously to combine. Shake well before use.

LEMON DRESSING

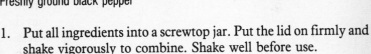

1 tablespoonful fresh lemon juice
3 tablespoonsful sunflower oil
1 heaped teaspoonful raw cane sugar
Freshly ground black pepper

1. Put all ingredients into a screwtop jar. Put the lid on firmly and shake vigorously to combine. Shake well before use.

SALAD DRESSING

2 level teaspoonsful soya flour
1 tablespoonful wine or cider vinegar
4 tablespoonsful sunflower oil
1/2 teaspoonful made English mustard
2 teaspoonsful raw cane sugar

1. Press the soya flour with the back of a spoon to get the lumps out.

2. Mix in a cup with the vinegar. Put into a screwtop jar with the rest of the ingredients and shake well to combine. Store in the fridge.

3. Shake well before using.

SALADS
Here is a selection of salads that all contain dried fruit and suggested dressings from the three recipes given. The approach I have taken

is to show off the colour of the salad with the dried fruit as a contrast.

A range of different coloured salads makes an eye-catching table decoration for a party. Put them in a bowl down the centre of the table as a feature of a cold buffet.

WHITE SALAD

White turnip, coarsely grated
White part of spring onions (scallions), finely chopped
White cabbage, shredded
Cauliflower, chopped
Raisins or chopped stoned dates (garnish)

Dress with French Dressing (page 34). Serve in a dark coloured bowl.

RED SALAD

Red cabbage, shredded
Tomatoes, chopped
Raw beetroot (beet), finely grated
Red pepper, de-seeded and finely chopped
Grated carrot (optional)
Chopped, stoned prunes (garnish)

Dress with French Dressing (page 34) and serve in a white bowl.

GREEN SALAD

Lettuce, torn into pieces
Cress
Watercress, in sprigs
Young spinach leaves, torn into pieces
Sultanas (golden seedless raisins) (garnish)

Use French or Lemon Dressing (page 35). Serve in a white bowl.

ORANGE SALAD

Grated carrot
Slices of orange
Grated swede (rutabaga)
Onion, finely chopped (garnish)
Chopped, stoned dates (garnish)

Dress with Lemon Dressing (page 35). Serve in a white or coloured bowl.

YELLOW SALAD

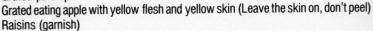

Yellow lettuce heart, shredded
Yellow pepper, de-seeded and chopped finely
Grated parsnip
Grated eating apple with yellow flesh and yellow skin (Leave the skin on, don't peel)
Raisins (garnish)

Dress with Lemon Dressing (page 35) as it will help to keep the apple from discolouring. Serve in a dark coloured bowl.

PALE GREEN SALAD

Raw Brussels sprouts, shredded (optional)
Chopped celery
Sliced cucumber
Granny Smith eating apple, grated (or other sweet green apple. Grate the skin as well.)
Shredded pale green cabbage heart, e.g. Savoy
Chopped dried apricots (garnish)

Dress with Lemon Dressing (page 35).

DARK GREEN SALAD

Tender leaves of curly kale, shredded
Young florets of calabrese (also leaves)
Watercress sprigs
Cos lettuce, torn into pieces
Raisins

Rub the bowl with a cut clove of garlic before making this salad. Dress with French Dressing (page 34). This salad looks beautiful in a white bowl.

PINK SALAD

Radishes, sliced
Button mushrooms, sliced
Beansprouts, chopped
Fresh pear, chopped (optional)
Chopped onion (garnish)
Cooked beetroot, chopped (garnish)
Chopped, stoned dates (garnish)

Dress with Lemon Dressing (page 34) and mix well. The vegetables (and the pear) will take up the colour of the beetroot and everything will be pink. Serve in a dark coloured bowl or a white one.

Mixed Salads

Start with a base of either torn lettuce pieces or shredded cabbage. Add something crunchy such as chopped celery, green or red peppers, or cauliflower. Grate or chop something moist like carrots or tomatoes. Sprinkle with dried fruit as a garnish — chopped apricots, stoned prunes, peaches, sultanas or raisins. To really give it a good flavour add a little chopped spring onion (scallion) or ordinary onion in thin rings. Dress with French, Lemon or Salad Dressing (see recipes page 34-5) and serve in a bowl.

Each season of the year brings different salad vegetables so there is no excuse for boredom! Winter salads are just as interesting as summer ones and the following one is my winter favourite:

WINTER SALAD I

Cauliflower, chopped
Tender leaves of curly kale or calabrese, shredded finely
Coarsely grated carrot
Raisins (garnish)

Dress with Lemon Dressing (page 35) and serve in a dark green or coloured bowl.

WINTER SALAD II

Chopped celery
Grated eating apple with skin left on
Coarsely grated carrot
Sultanas (golden seedless raisins) (garnish)

Dress with Lemon Dressing (page 35).

PEPPER SALAD

Mix green and red, chopped, de-seeded peppers. Garnish with chopped, stoned dates. Dress with French or Lemon Dressing (page 35). (Also use the multicoloured or more unusual coloured peppers such as black and yellow, if available.)

MIXED ROOT SALAD

Grated carrot
Grated swede (rutabaga) or white turnip
Grated or sliced radish (garnish)
Chopped spring onions (scallions) (garnish)
Chopped stoned dates (garnish)

Dress with French Dressing (page 34).

MIXED LETTUCE SALAD

Use 3 or 4 kinds of lettuce torn into small pieces. Garnish with chopped spring onion (scallion) or thinly sliced onion rings and chopped, stoned dates. A sprinkle of freshly chopped parsley will round off the taste. Dress with French Dressing (page 34).

4.

DESSERTS

DRIED FRUIT WHIP
Serves 3 to 4

A very easily made, simple sweet. Use stoned prunes, dried apricots, peaches or pears, or any mixture of dried fruits for the fruit purée.

Imperial (Metric)	American
¾ pint (425ml) thick fruit purée, (cooked) and sweetened with raw cane sugar	2 cupsful thick fruit purée (cooked) and sweetened with raw cane sugar
Finely grated rind of 1 lemon	Finely grated rind of 1 lemon
2 egg whites	2 egg whites

1. Allow fruit purée to cool and stir in the lemon rind.

2. Whip egg whites until they will stand in peaks.

3. Fold into the cold fruit purée with a metal spoon.

4. Put into glass dishes and chill in the fridge.

DRIED FRUIT SUNDAE
Put alternate layers of stewed and sweetened apricots, double (heavy) cream, and crushed digestive biscuits (Graham crackers) into tall glasses. Top with a sprinkle of nuts, or half a stewed apricot.

Other dried fruits can be used — prunes, figs or fruit salad.

DRIED FRUIT SOUFFLÉ
Serves 6

For the fruit in this recipe use either apricots, nectarines, stoned prunes, pears or peaches.

Imperial (Metric)	American
½ lb (225g) dried fruit	1½ cupsful dried fruit
Water	Water
Juice of 1 lemon	Juice of 1 lemon
2 oz (55g) raw cane sugar	⅓ cupful raw cane sugar
3 egg whites	3 egg whites

1. Soak the dried fruit overnight in water and the lemon juice.

2. The next day add a little more water and the sugar and bring to the boil. Simmer for 20 to 30 minutes until the fruit is soft enough to liquidize. Allow to cool.

3. Put the fruit mixture into the blender and pour off most of the juice. Reserve this for later.

4. Liquidize to a smooth purée and turn into a basin.

5. Beat the egg whites until stiff and then fold into the fruit mixture. Put into a buttered soufflé dish.

6. Bake in a preheated oven at 350°F/180°C (Gas Mark 4), above the centre of the oven for about 25 minutes.

7. Serve immediately it comes out of the oven, with what is left of the cooking juices poured over as a sauce.

Note: This can be baked in 6 individual soufflé dishes for approx. 20 minutes.

ORANGE DESSERT
Serve slices of orange, sprinkled with raw cane sugar and a garnish of chopped stoned dates. This looks tempting in a glass dish on a stem. A very simple but delicious sweet.

BAKED STUFFED APPLES

Serves 1

Imperial (Metric)	**American**
1 large cooking apple	1 large cooking apple
Stuffing (from list below)	Stuffing (from list below)
Water	Water
Raw cane sugar	Raw cane sugar

1. Preheat oven at 350°F/180°C (Gas Mark 4).

2. Wash apple but do not peel. Cut a line round the middle, through the skin.

3. Remove core with apple corer and discard.

4. Put into an ovenproof dish and put stuffing into the centre cavity with a teaspoon.

5. Pour a cupful of water into the dish and sprinkle the apple with sugar.

6. Bake above centre of the oven for about 30 minutes.

7. Serve hot or cold with the juice from the dish.

Stuffings:

a) Home-made mincemeat.

b) Home-made almond paste and a chopped stoned date.

c) Sultanas (golden seedless raisins).

d) Raisins.

e) Chopped dried apricots (about 2 or 3 halves) and lemon rind.

Variations: Instead of cooking in water try milk with 2 or 3 pinches of cinnamon. Instead of sugar trail black treacle (molasses) over the apple in circles.

JAMAICAN BANANAS
Serves 4-6

Imperial (Metric)
2 oz (55g) polyunsaturated
　margarine
4 to 6 bananas, peeled
2 oz (55g) raw cane sugar
Pinch of cinnamon
8 dates, stoned and sliced
1 tablespoonful rum

American
¼ cupful polyunsaturated margarine
4 to 6 bananas, peeled
⅓ cupful raw cane sugar
Pinch of cinnamon
8 dates, stoned and sliced
1 tablespoonful rum

1. Use a large frying pan (skillet) to melt the margarine.

2. Cut the bananas lengthways and put into the pan.

3. Sprinkle with the sugar, spice and dates.

4. Fry gently for a few seconds, then turn the bananas over to cook on the other side.

5. Take off the heat and allow to cool for 5 minutes.

6. Spoon over the rum and reheat.

7. Serve immediately with a little single (light) cream.

Note: A quickly made sweet. If the heat is too fierce when you reheat the rum it may ignite, so do it gently.

BAKED BANANAS

Imperial (Metric)
4 large bananas
1 heaped tablespoonful raw cane
　sugar
Grated rind and juice of 1 orange
1 level tablespoonful raisins

American
4 large bananas
1 heaped tablespoonful raw cane
　sugar
Grated rind and juice of 1 orange
1 level tablespoonful raisins

1. Preheat oven at 325°F/160°C (Gas Mark 3).

2. Grease an ovenproof dish.

3. Peel the bananas and slice lengthways.

4. Place in the dish and sprinkle with the orange rind, juice and raisins.

5. Bake above centre of the oven for about 30 minutes and serve hot.

Variation: Omit orange juice and rind and use 2 tablespoonsful pineapple juice instead.

DRIED FRUIT JELLY
Serves 4

Imperial (Metric)	American
4 oz (115g) dried apricots, pears, peaches or stoned prunes	²/₃ cupful dried apricots, pears, peaches or stoned prunes
Water	Water
Raw cane sugar to taste	Raw cane sugar to taste
1 level teaspoonful agar-agar	1 slightly heaped teaspoonful agar-agar

1. Soak the fruit overnight in cold water.

2. The next day, cook for about 20 minutes. Cool a little.

3. Liquidize and add raw cane sugar to taste.

4. The liquid should measure ½ pint/285ml (1⅓ cupsful). Make it up to this level with water if necessary.

5. Bring the juice to the boil to dissolve the sugar. Sprinkle in the agar-agar and stir until that too has dissolved.

6. Pour into 2 or 3 glass dishes and leave to set.

7. Serve chilled from the fridge on the day of making.

Variations: Add the juice of ½ a lemon or orange before liquidizing. Serve with home-made vanilla ice cream.

FRUIT TRIFLE

This recipe serves 4 and can be made in a glass serving bowl or 4 individual dishes. A most attractive sweet for special occasions.

Base:

Imperial (Metric)	American
2 sponge buns	2 sponge buns
Raw sugar jam	Raw sugar jelly
1 large almond macaroon	1 large almond macaroon
Juice of 1 orange	Juice of 1 orange
3 tablespoonsful sweet sherry	3 tablespoonsful sweet sherry
1 heaped teaspoonful raisins	1 heaped teaspoonful raisins
8 cooked, dried apricots	8 cooked, dried apricots
1 oz (30g) chopped almonds	1 heaped tablespoonful chopped almonds

Topping (Real Custard):

Imperial (Metric)	American
1 large egg	1 large egg
1 egg yolk	1 egg yolk
2 oz (55g) raw cane sugar	⅓ cupful raw cane sugar
¾ pint (425ml) warm milk	2 cupsful warm milk
Few drops pure vanilla flavouring	Few drops pure vanilla flavouring

Decoration:

Imperial (Metric)	American
Ratafias (miniature almond macaroons)	Ratafias (miniature almond macaroons)
Toasted, flaked almonds	Toasted, slivered almonds

1. Make the base. Split the sponge cakes and sandwich with jam (jelly).

2. Put into a glass serving dish after cutting each one into four.

3. Break the macaroon into pieces and add to the dish.

4. Pour over the orange juice and sherry, then sprinkle with the fruit and nuts.

5. Make the real custard topping. Beat the egg with the egg yolk and sugar. Stir in the warm milk.

6. Pour into a double saucepan or use a basin over a pan of hot water. Cook gently while you stir until the custard thickens and coats the back of the wooden stirring spoon.

7. Allow to cool a little and then pour over the base.

8. Leave to grow cold and set. Decorate with the little ratafias and sprinkle with the toasted almonds.

DRIED FRUIT SALAD
Soak fruit salad overnight in water. The next day bring to the boil in a saucepan, adding more water if needed. Add raw cane sugar to taste and a little lemon juice or finely grated rind of a lemon. Simmer for about 30 minutes until all the fruit is tender. Serve on its own, hot or cold with a little single (light) cream or real custard. Can also be stewed in the oven after bringing to the boil on the top of the stove. Use a flameproof casserole with a lid. It will take up to 2 hours in a very low oven or about an hour in a moderately hot one.

FRUIT SALAD
Perk up a fresh fruit salad with a few raisins or sultanas (golden seedless raisins) soaked in sweet sherry for an hour.

UNCOOKED, DRIED FRUIT SALAD
Soak for 36 hours in cold water. Sweeten to taste when you drain and serve. This method doesn't provide such a good juice as when it is cooked, so you might like to serve it in pineapple or orange juice, sweetened with raw cane sugar.

LEBANESE FRUIT SALAD
Serves 3 to 4

Imperial (Metric)
1 fresh melon, preferably Ogen
2 tablespoonsful orange liqueur
1 tablespoonful rosewater
3 tablespoonsful runny honey
¼ pint (140ml) warm water
4 dried figs, chopped and soaked
8 dates, stoned and halved
1 tablespoonful raisins
1 tablespoonful chopped almonds
1 tablespoonful chopped walnuts

American
1 fresh melon, preferably Ogen
2 tablespoonsful orange liqueur
1 tablespoonful rosewater
3 tablespoonsful runny honey
⅔ cupful warm water
4 dried figs, chopped and soaked
8 dates, stoned and halved
1 tablespoonful raisins
1 tablespoonful chopped almonds
1 generous tablespoonful chopped English walnuts

1. Put the melon into the fridge to chill.

2. Pour the liqueur, rosewater, honey and warm water into a bowl. Mix well to blend.

3. Put in the fruit and nuts. Mix well.

4. Leave covered in the fridge for 2 to 3 hours.

5. Cut the chilled melon in half and remove the seeds with a spoon. Slice into wedges and cut off the flesh. Chop into cubes.

6. Mix the melon with the fruit salad and serve chilled from the fridge.

Note: Leave the skins on the almonds, i.e. don't blanch them.

STEWED FRUITS
Stew fresh apple with water and raw cane sugar to taste plus a sprinkle of raisins or sultanas (golden seedless raisins). Makes a change from just plain stewed apple. You can also add a pinch or two of powdered cloves.

FRUIT CREAMS
Serves 4-6

For the dried fruit choose from apricots, stoned prunes, peaches or pears.

Imperial (Metric)	American
½ lb (225g) dried fruit	1½ cupsful dried fruit
¼ pint (140ml) plain yogurt	⅔ cupful plain yogurt
2 tablespoonsful single cream	2 tablespoonsful light cream
2 tablespoonsful fresh lemon juice	3 teaspoonsful fresh lemon juice
2 bananas, peeled and sliced	2 bananas, peeled and sliced
Raw cane sugar or honey to taste	Raw cane sugar or honey to taste
Toasted, flaked almonds for decoration	Toasted, slivered almonds to taste

1. Soak the fruit of your choice overnight, in cold water.

2. Put the soaked dried fruit, yogurt, cream, lemon juice, bananas into a liquidizer and blend.

3. Add sweetening to taste and stir in.

4. Spoon into glass dishes and chill in the fridge.

5. Serve straight from the fridge, sprinkled with the toasted almonds.

Note: For anyone hooked on the kind of instant dessert that comes out of a packet to be mixed with milk, this dessert could wean you off the junk variety. Don't make them too sweet. A slightly tart dessert is always refreshing.

STUFFED PRUNES DESSERT
Soak and cook prunes in the usual way. Put a walnut (English walnut) half in each one instead of the stone and put back into a generous pan of juice to soak a little more. Serve with sponge fingers or ginger biscuits. The juice can be enriched with lemon juice, orange juice, a little sweet sherry or red wine.

DRIED FRUIT COMPOTE
Serves 4

Imperial (Metric)	American
½ lb (225g) dried fruit salad	2 cupsful dried fruit salad
2 oz (55g) dried figs or nectarines	⅓ cupful dried figs or nectarines
1 oz (30g) raisins	1 heaped tablespoonful raisins
⅓ pint (200ml) water	¾ cupful water
5 tablespoonsful red wine	5 tablespoonsful red wine
Coarsely grated rind of 1 lemon (small)	Coarsely grated rind of 1 lemon (small)
¾ teaspoonful cinnamon	¾ teaspoonsful cinnamon
4 oz (115g) raw cane sugar	⅔ cupful raw cane sugar

1. Soak the dried fruit overnight in cold water.

2. Make the juice. Put the water, wine, lemon rind, cinnamon and sugar in a saucepan. Bring to the boil and stir until the sugar has dissolved.

3. Drain the fruit and add to the pan. Cool for about 20 minutes until the fruit is tender.

4. Drain the fruit and reserve the juice. If you are serving hot, keep the fruit warm in a low oven.

5. Boil the juice for about 15 minutes to reduce it and it turns into a rich syrup.

6. Pour over the fruit in a glass serving dish.

7. Serve hot or allow to cool and serve chilled from the fridge.

Note: A very simple, attractive sweet as the wine intensifies the colour of the dried fruit. The lemon rind can be thinly pared and cut into long, thin strips if preferred.

DRIED FRUIT MOUSSE
Serves 6

This is made with the same ingredients as the Dried Fruit Soufflé (page 42) and by following the method down to point 4. Then proceed as follows:

5. Turn into a bowl and fold in ¼ pint/140ml (⅔ cupful) beaten whipping cream (heavy cream).

6. Fold in the stiffly beaten egg whites. Put into a soufflé dish and chill in the fridge.

7. Serve the same day, straight from the fridge.

5.

PUDDINGS

BATTER PUDDING
Serves 3 or 4

Batter:

Imperial (Metric)	American
2 oz (55g) wholemeal flour	½ cupful wholewheat flour
1 egg	1 egg
Pinch of sea salt	Pinch of sea salt
¼ pint (140ml) milk	⅔ cupful milk

Filling etc:

Imperial (Metric)	American
1 tablespoonful vegetable oil	1 tablespoonful vegetable oil
2 oz (55g) currants	⅓ cupful currants
Raw cane sugar or liquid honey	Raw cane sugar or liquid honey

1. Put the flour into a bowl and make a well in the centre.

2. Break in the egg and stir. This will give you lumps and loose flour but don't worry at this stage.

3. Add the milk, a little at a time, mixing thoroughly. As soon as the mixture can be beaten, beat energetically to get the lumps out.

4. Add more milk and beat again until you have a thin, smooth batter. Leave to stand for an hour, if you have the time.

5. Preheat oven to 475°F/240°C (Gas Mark 9).

6. Put the oil into a baking tin and put over a medium heat until it begins to smoke slightly. (If prefered put it into the oven to heat.)

7. Stir the fruit into the batter and pour quickly into the hot tin.

8. Put straight into the preheated oven on the top shelf.

9. After about 5 or 6 minutes turn down the heat to 400°F/200°C (Gas Mark 6) and bake for another 30 to 35 minutes, or, until the pudding has risen and you know the middle to be cooked.

10. Serve immediately on hot plates, with raw cane sugar or honey to taste.

Note: Time this popular pudding to be ready when you want to eat it, as a delay will allow it to collapse into a miserable, leathery disaster. Yorkshire pudding fans will appreciate this delicacy and children usually adore it. It is best made with currants as they contrast well with the batter. It has a good protein and fibre content as well as being not too sweet. I do know someone who has this every Sunday for breakfast . . .

APPLE SLICES
Serves 3 or 4

This recipe comes from Spain, where it is served as a snack or pudding. If you don't have any fresh mint leaves to chop, use ½ level teaspoonful dried mint. Dried cardamom can be used instead of crushing a seed but the cost in the UK is really prohibitive.

Imperial (Metric)
4 oz (115g) wholemeal flour
2 oz (55g) polyunsaturated margarine
2 heaped tablespoonsful raw cane sugar
Few drops pure vanilla flavouring
1 egg, beaten
1 lb (455g) cooking apples
2 leaves fresh mint, finely chopped
1 level teaspoonful cinnamon
1 cardamom seed, crushed in a pestle and mortar
1 heaped tablespoonful sultanas

American
1 cupful wholewheat flour
¼ cupful polyunsaturated margarine
2 heaped tablespoonsful raw cane sugar
Few drops pure vanilla flavouring
1 egg, beaten
1 pound cooking apples
2 leaves fresh mint, finely chopped
1 level teaspoonful cinnamon
1 cardamom seed, crushed in a pestle and mortar
1 heaped tablespoonful golden seedless raisins

1. Preheat oven at 425°F/220°C (Gas Mark 7).

2. Put the flour into a bowl with the margarine. Rub in with the fingers until the mixture resembles breadcrumbs.

3. Stir in the sugar and vanilla flavouring.

4. Add about half the beaten egg and mix to a soft dough. (Add a little water, if needed.)

5. Peel the apples, core them and cut into thin slices. Put into a basin with the mint, spices and dried fruit. Mix well.

6. Roll about two thirds of the pastry thinly to line a small sponge tin or ovenproof dish.

7. Fill with the apple mixture and wet the edge of the pastry.

8. Roll out the remaining pastry to make the lid. Cover the filling and press the edges together to seal. Trim off excess with a knife and prick all over with a fork.

9. Brush the top with the rest of the beaten egg and bake above centre of the oven for about 40 to 45 minutes.

10. Cool a little before you take it out of the tin.

Note: Best served still warm from the oven, cut into slices.

BAKED FRUIT BATTER

Imperial (Metric)
4 small cooking apples, peeled and quartered
2 heaped tablespoonsful sultanas
Raw cane sugar
1 tablespoonful vegetable oil
Batter (see Batter Pudding recipe, (page 52)

American
4 small cooking apples, peeled and quartered
2 heaped tablespoonsful golden seedless raisins
Raw cane sugar
1 tablespoonful vegetable oil
Batter (see Batter Pudding recipe, page 52)

1. Preheat oven at 425°F/220°C (Gas Mark 7).

2. Put the oil in a roasting tin and heat until a faint blue haze appears.

3. Remove from heat and put in the apple quarters. Sprinkle with sugar. Do this quickly as the tin must be kept hot.

4. Sprinkle in the sultanas (golden seedless raisins).

5. Pour the batter over the fruit and put straight into the oven.

6. Bake for about 30 minutes until the apples are baked and the sultanas plump.

7. Serve immediately on hot plates.

Note: A good recipe when you have cooking apples that are too small to bake whole. A little mixed spice or cinnamon can be sprinkled into the batter before it is poured over the fruit. Serve with top of the milk or single (light) cream to make it special.

FRUIT COBBLER

Serves 6-8

Fruit:

Imperial (Metric)	American
¾ lb (340g) dried fruit salad	2½ cupsful dried fruit salad
3 oz (85g) raw cane sugar	½ cupful raw cane sugar

Topping:

Imperial (Metric)	American
½ lb (225g) wholemeal flour	2 cupsful wholewheat flour
1 teaspoonful baking powder	1 teaspoonful baking powder
3 oz (85g) polyunsaturated margarine	⅓ cupful polyunsaturated margarine
4 tablespoonsful milk	4 tablespoonsful milk
1 egg, beaten	1 egg, beaten

1. Soak the dried fruit overnight and cook for 20 minutes with enough water to allow the fruit to swell, and sweeten with the sugar.

2. Preheat oven at 400°F/200°C (Gas Mark 6).

3. Grease a 2 pint (1.1 litre) pie dish and arrange the cooked fruit in this.

4. Put into the oven to warm while you make the topping.

5. Put the flour into the mixing bowl and sprinkle in the baking powder. Mix well.

6. Add the margarine and rub in until the mixture resembles breadcrumbs.

7. Sprinkle in the sugar. Stir and make a well in the centre.

8. Mix the milk with the egg and pour into the well. Use a fork to combine into a dough.

9. Sprinkle the worktop with flour and roll out the dough thickly — ½ in. (1cm).

10. Flour a crinkle-edged cutter and cut into about 8 or 9 rounds.

11. Place around the pie dish, over the fruit, overlapping them neatly.

12. Bake above centre for 15 to 20 minutes, then turn down the heat to 375°F/190°C (Gas Mark 5) for another 10 minutes.

13. Serve hot from the oven with single (light) cream, real custard or home-made ice-cream.

BREAD AND 'BUTTER' PUDDING
Serves 3 to 4

Imperial (Metric)

6 slices wholemeal bread, spread
    with polyunsaturated margarine
3 oz (85g) seedless raisins
½ teaspoonful grated nutmeg
2 tablespoonsful raw cane sugar
2 eggs
¾ pint (425ml) milk

American

6 slices wholewheat bread, spread
    with polyunsaturated margarine
¾ cupful seedless raisins
½ teaspoonful grated nutmeg
2 tablespoonsful raw cane sugar
2 eggs
2 cupsful milk

1. Grease a shallow baking dish.

2. Remove crusts from bread and discard. Cut into quarters.

3. Place a layer (with spread side down) over the bottom of the dish.

4. Sprinkle with half the raisins, half the nutmeg and half the sugar.

5. Cover with another layer of bread quarters and sprinkle with the remaining raisins, nutmeg and sugar.

6. Top with a layer of bread, spread side up.

7. Beat the eggs with the milk.

8. Strain over the bread and leave for 30 minutes or so to allow the bread to soak up the milk mixture.

9. Preheat oven 375°F/190°C (Gas Mark 5).

10. Bake the pudding on the middle shelf for about 45 minutes.

11. Serve hot from the oven, crisp and golden brown.

Variations: Sultanas (golden seedless raisins) or currants will do instead of raisins. Cinnamon or mixed spice may be used instead of the nutmeg. For a more 'custardy' flavour add a few drops of vanilla flavouring to the milk and egg mixture.

Glamour cooks have done much to spoil this traditional British pudding by using white bread instead of wholemeal , butter instead of margarine, cream instead of milk and too much white sugar. Try this wholefood version for maximum nutrition and high-fibre. A semi-sweet pudding that is very filling and substantial. Good for cold winter days.

DRIED FRUIT CRUMBLE
Serves 4

Topping:

Imperial (Metric)	American
4 oz (115g) wholemeal flour	1 cupful wholewheat flour
2 oz (55g) polyunsaturated margarine	¼ cupful polyunsaturated margarine
2 heaped teaspoonsful sesame seeds	2 heaped teaspoonsful sesame seeds
2 heaped teaspoonsful sunflower seeds	2 heaped teaspoonsful sunflower seeds
1 heaped teaspoonful raw cane sugar	1 heaped teaspoonful raw cane sugar

Base:

Imperial (Metric)	American
4 servings stewed, dried fruit (see note on Stewed Fruit page 18)	4 servings stewed, dried fruit (see note on Stewed Fruit page 18)

1. Put the flour into a mixing bowl. Rub in the margarine.

2. Use a fork to stir in the sesame seeds, sunflower seeds and the sugar.

3. Half-fill an ovenproof dish with the stewed fruit of your choice.

4. Sprinkle with the topping in a thick layer and bake in a preheated oven at 450°F/230°C (Gas Mark 8) for 10 to 12 minutes.

5. Serve on warm plates with single (light) cream.

Note: This is a quickly baked pudding that provides plenty of fibre in the topping. Vary the flavour with different kinds of fruit — prune, apricot, fruit salad, peach, etc.

CHRISTMAS PLUM PUDDING

This pudding is as English as they come. It is traditionally eaten on Christmas Day and the days following Christmas until it is all finished up. Most people tend to buy their Christmas Pudding at the supermarket thinking it will be too difficult for them to make at home. I have never yet tasted a commercially-made one that could hold a candle to a home-made one and although the list of ingredients is somewhat daunting in its length, it is a very simple pudding that can be made weeks in advance. This version is made without beef suet, (the traditional source of fat for this type of pudding), and will serve 6 to 8 people.

Imperial (Metric)	American
2 oz (55g) wholemeal flour	½ cupful wholewheat flour
1 level teaspoonful each of:	1 slightly heaped teaspoonful of:
nutmeg	nutmeg
cinnamon	cinnamon
mixed spice	mixed spice
2 oz (55g) each of:	½ cupful wholewheat flour
wholemeal flour	¼ cupful melted margarine
melted margarine	⅓ cupful each of:
raw cane sugar	raw cane sugar
grated apple	grated apple
grated fresh carrot	grated fresh carrot
chopped, dried apricots	chopped, dried apricots
currants	currants
sultanas	golden seedless raisins
chopped, stoned prunes	chopped, stoned prunes
chopped almonds	chopped almonds
1 oz (30g) wholemeal breadcrumbs	2 heaped tablespoonful wholewheat breadcrumbs
4 oz (115g) raisins	⅔ cupful raisins
1 tablespoonful black treacle	1 tablespoonful molasses
4 tablespoonsful ale or beer or brandy	4 tablespoonsful ale, beer or brandy
1 egg	1 egg
Coarsely grated rind of 1 lemon and 1 orange	Coarsely grated rind of 1 lemon and 1 orange

| Juice of 1 lemon and 1 orange | Juice of 1 lemon and 1 orange |
| 2 teaspoonsful soya sauce | 2 teaspoonsful soy sauce |

1. Mix the ingredients in a mixing bowl and leave overnight.

2. The following day stir well and put into a greased basin. Cover with a round of greaseproof paper, greased on both sides, and cover, sealing tightly. (See Chapter 1, page 17, for instructions.)

3. Steam gently for about 6 hours.

4. Allow to grow cold and put on new covers. The pudding can now be stored in a cool dry place for several weeks until needed.

5. On Christmas Day steam again for about 2 hours and serve hot with brandy butter or real custard. (Children will prefer the custard.)

Note: Make the brandy butter by creaming 4 oz (115g) butter with 3 oz (85g) raw cane sugar and 1 tablespoonful of brandy. (The American measures are: ½ cupful each of butter and raw cane sugar and 1⅓ tablespoonsful brandy.)

APRICOT UPSIDEDOWN PUDDING
Serves 6-8

Topping:

Imperial (Metric)	American
Butter	Butter
2 oz (55g) raw cane sugar	⅓ cupful raw cane sugar
½ lb (225g) cooked dried apricots	1⅓ cupsful cooked, dried apricots

Base:

Imperial (Metric)	American
4 oz (115g) polyunsaturated margarine	½ cupful polyunsaturated margarine
4 oz (115g) raw cane sugar	⅔ cupful raw cane sugar
5 oz (140g) wholemeal flour	1¼ cupsful wholewheat flour
1 level teaspoonful baking powder	1 level teaspoonful baking powder
2 eggs, beaten	2 eggs, beaten

1. Liberally grease (with butter) a shallow ovenproof dish with straight sides, about the size of a sponge tin.

2. Sprinkle all over with the raw cane sugar and arrange the cooked apricots in a pattern.

3. Preheat the oven at 375°F/190°C (Gas Mark 5).

4. Put all ingredients for the base into a mixing bowl and mix to a creamy consistency.

5. Carefully spoon the base mixture over the fruit, making sure that you fill all the spaces. Level off with a knife.

6. Bake above centre for about 25 minutes.

7. Cool on a wire rack.

8. When required, put a plate over the pudding. Hold the two firmly together and turn upside down. Shake the pudding on to the plate and remove the dish.

9. Decorate with rosettes of whipped cream to make it special.

Variation: Other kinds of fruit can be used and made into a pattern. Make sure you put the fruit into the dish with the cut sides uppermost.

BAKED APRICOT CUSTARD
Serves 4-5

Imperial (Metric)	American
6 oz (140g) dried apricots	1 cupful dried apricots
3 eggs	3 eggs
3 tablespoonsful raw cane sugar	3 tablespoonsful raw cane sugar
1 pint (570ml) milk	2½ cupsful milk

1. Soak the fruit overnight in cold water.

2. Preheat oven at 350°F/180°C (Gas Mark 4).

3. Beat the eggs with the sugar, then add the milk and beat again.

4. Put the drained apricots into a greased ovenproof dish and pour the milk mixture over them.

5. Place the dish in a roasting pan of warm water and put into the oven above centre.

6. Bake for about 1½ hours, until the custard has set.

7. Serve hot or cold.

Variation: Just as good with dried pears, peaches, nectarines and stoned prunes.

STEAMED PUDDING

As vegetarians don't use suet (beef fat), suet pastry is not on the menu. However, here is a pastry I have invented which is very similar in appearance and taste, made from quite different ingredients and with half the fat. A substantial, rib-sticking hot pudding to serve 3 or 4.

Pastry:

Imperial (Metric)	American
2 oz (55g) polyunsaturated margarine	¼ cupful polyunsaturated margarine
4 oz (115g) ground rice	½ cupful ground rice
3 oz (85g) eating apple, grated	1 eating apple, grated

Filling:

Imperial (Metric)	American
2 large portions dried fruit (about 4-5 oz)	2 large portions dried fruit (about 4-5 ounces)
Raw cane sugar to taste	Raw cane sugar to taste

1. Soak the fruit overnight in cold water.

2. Make the pastry. Put the margarine, ground rice and grated apple into a bowl and blend with a fork. Make into a stiff paste by kneading with the fingers, using more ground rice if the mixture is too sticky.

3. Grease a 1 pint/570ml (2½ cupful) pudding basin and liberally grease with margarine.

4. Take two-thirds of the pastry dough and roll into a ball. Flatten and put into the bottom of the basin. Press out with your fingers so that it lines the sides of the basin. Try to do this evenly and so that the pastry extends to just ½ in. (1cm) below the rim of the basin.

5. Make the remaining one third of the pastry into a flat circle for the lid.

6. Spoon the fruit, with a little of the juice, into the pastry and sprinkle with the sugar. The pastry should be filled almost to the top.

7. Use a spatula to place the pastry lid on top and press the edges to seal them on to the bottom part.

8. Steam for 45 minutes, after tying on a greaseproof paper cover. (See page 16 for instructions on steaming.)

9. When ready, take the basin out of the saucepan by its string handle. Remove cover and string. Put a warmed plate over the top of the basin and hold the two firmly together while you turn them upside down. Don't be tempted to shake the pudding but just leave it for a few seconds to drop gently on to the plate. Lift off the basin carefully.

10. Serve hot on its own or with real custard. (See Fruit Trifle recipe, page 46.)

Note: For the fruit use dried fruit salad, or prunes, dried apricots, peaches and pears. Half a teaspoonful of cinnamon can be added to the fruit salad, apricots or pears. The grated rind of a lemon can be added to the prunes or the apricots for variation. Figs can also be used, but the combination of the apple pastry and the figs might prove a little devastating for some people!

SPOTTED DICK
Serves 4 to 6

There are several variations of Spotted Dick but all feature currants in some kind of steamed base. It does not need to be boiled in a pudding cloth but can be steamed slowly in a basin, as in this new recipe.

Imperial (Metric)	American
4 oz (115g) wholemeal flour	1 cupful wholewheat flour
1½ teaspoonsful baking powder	1½ teaspoonsful baking powder
3 oz (85g) polyunsaturated margarine	⅓ cupful polyunsaturated margarine
2 oz (55g) raw cane sugar	⅓ cupful raw cane sugar
4 oz (115g) currants	⅔ cupful currants
1 small cooking apple, finely grated	1 small cooking apple, finely grated
3 oz (85g) wholemeal breadcrumbs	1½ slices wholewheat breadcrumbs
Finely grated rind of 1 lemon	Finely grated rind of 1 lemon
Milk to mix	Milk to mix

1. Put the flour into a bowl with the baking powder and mix well. Blend in the margarine with a fork, as well as you can.

2. Stir in the sugar, currants, grated apple, breadcrumbs and lemon rind. Mix well.

3. Add enough milk to make a soft dropping consistency.

4. Grease a 1½ pint (850ml) pudding basin and spoon the mixture into it.

5. Cover with a piece of greased, greaseproof paper, grease side downwards. Tie on a lid and handle. (See page 16 for notes on steaming.)

6. Steam for about 2 hours, topping up with more hot water as required.

7. Turn out on to a plate. Serve hot with real custard.

Note: Although the texture is coarse the pudding is light and lemony. A very lightweight version of a traditional pudding.

APRICOT CRUMBLE

Base:

Imperial (Metric)	American
4 portions soaked and stewed dried apricots sweetened to taste with raw cane sugar	4 portions soaked and stewed dried apricots sweetened to taste with raw cane sugar
¼ teaspoonful cinnamon	¼ teaspoonful cinnamon

Topping:

Imperial (Metric)	American
3 oz (85g) wholemeal flour	¾ cupful wholewheat flour
2 oz (55g) polyunsaturated margarine	¼ cupful polyunsaturated margarine
1 oz (30g) raw cane sugar	2½ heaped tablespoonsful raw cane sugar

1. Preheat oven at 400°F/200°C (Gas Mark 6).

2. Put the base into an ovenproof dish and stir in the spice.

3. Make the topping. Put the flour into a bowl with the margarine and rub in with the fingers until the mixture resembles fine breadcrumbs.

4. Stir in the sugar.

5. Sprinkle the topping over the fruit and bake in the centre of the oven for about 15 minutes.

6. Lower the heat to 375°F/190°C (Gas Mark 5) and bake for another 15 minutes.

Note: A very simple dish. The apricots should be slightly tart, i.e. not too sweet. The topping is a semi-sweet one. On special occasions serve with single (light) cream.

Variation: Instead of dried apricots, try dried pears.

LIGHT CHRISTMAS PUDDING

Make as for Spotted Dick (page 66) but vary the dried fruit and add ¼ teaspoonful each of: cinnamon, nutmeg and mixed spice, plus 1 tablespoonful black treacle (molasses) and a few chopped almonds. Also add a dash of brandy. Make on the day you want to eat it. For people who find the traditional Christmas Pudding too heavy and too rich.

SPONGE PUDDINGS WITH DRIED FRUIT

Basic Recipe

Imperial (Metric)	American
4 oz (115g) polyunsaturated margarine	½ cupful polyunsaturated margarine
4 oz (115g) raw cane sugar	⅔ cupful raw cane sugar
2 eggs	2 eggs
6 oz (170g) wholemeal flour	1½ cupsful wholewheat flour
1½ level teaspoonsful baking powder	2 level teaspoonsful baking powder
Flavouring (optional)	Flavouring (optional)
6 oz (170g) dried fruit (see list below of 10 suggestions)	1 cupful dried fruit (see list below of 10 suggestions)

1. Put the margarine into a bowl with the sugar and beat to a cream.

2. Beat in the eggs.

3. Stir in the flour and baking powder. If the mixture is too stiff, add a little cold milk and stir again. The mixture should be soft enough to drop from the spoon.

4. Add the flavouring (if any) and the dried fruit of your choice. Fold in gently.

5. Turn into a well greased pudding basin. The mixture should not come more than two-thirds of the way up the basin as it will rise during steaming.

6. Cover with greased greaseproof paper and then a double layer of greaseproof paper with a pleat. Tie on the lid with suitable string and steam for 1½ hours. (See page 16 for notes on steaming.)

7. Remove wrappers and place a hot dish over the top. Turn upside down and serve hot with real custard or just as it is.

For the dried fruit and flavouring add one of the following:
a) Grated rind of 1 lemon and sultanas (golden seedless raisins) or currants.
b) Grated rind of 1 orange and raisins.
c) Grated rind of 1 lemon and chopped, dried bananas.
d) Grated rind of 1 lemon and chopped, stoned prunes.
e) 1 oz/30g (1 heaped tablespoonful) carob powder with chopped, stoned dates.
f) Grated rind of 1 lemon with chopped dried apricots.
g) Mixture of currants, sultanas (golden seedless raisins) and raisins.
h) Chopped dried pears with 1 teaspoonful cinnamon or ground ginger.
i) Chopped dried peaches.
j) Chopped, dried fruit salad with either rind of an orange or lemon, grated finely.

Note: These puddings will serve about 6 people generously. Very popular with children who will appreciate the magic moment of turning the pudding out upside down on to a plate.

FRUIT PANCAKES

Like many simple dishes, absolutely delicious and easily made.

Batter:

Imperial (Metric)	American
2 eggs, beaten	2 eggs, beaten
4 oz (115g) wholemeal flour	1 cupful wholewheat flour
Approx. ½ pint (285ml) milk	Approx. 1⅓ cupsful milk
Vegetable oil for cooking	Vegetable oil for cooking

Filling:

Imperial (Metric)	American
1 lb (455g) cooking apples	1 pound cooking apples
Water	Water
Raw cane sugar to taste	Raw cane sugar to taste
1 tablespoonful raisins or sultanas, or chopped dates	1 tablespoonful raisins or golden seedless raisins, or chopped dates

1. Make the batter. Add the eggs to the flour and mix well in a bowl.

2. Gradually add the milk, a little at a time, beating out the lumps after each addition.

3. When all the milk has been added, beat well to make a smooth, thin batter. Pour into a jug.

4. Make the filling. Peel and core the apples. Slice thinly and put into a saucepan with a little water and sugar to stew.

5. Heat, while you stir, and cook until the apples can be mixed to a purée. Stir in the dried fruit. Keep hot, while you make the pancakes (crêpes).

6. Have a heated plate ready and a place to keep the pancakes (crêpes) warm until you are ready to serve.

7. Put about 2 teaspoonsful of vegetable oil into a frying pan (skillet). Heat and tip the pan to coat the surface. When the oil begins to make a slight haze, pour in enough pancake (crêpe) batter to

cover half the pan. Tip the pan so that the batter runs all over the base, making a thin covering.

8. Cook on one side, then turn (or toss if you are brave) to cook the other side. Transfer to the warmed plate and keep warm while you make the remaining batter into pancakes (crêpes).

9. When you have made them all, use half the apple mixture to spread over the pancakes (crêpes). Roll them up and top with the rest of the filling. Serve immediately, on warmed plates.

Note: If you would rather not serve them rolled, the pancakes can be stacked one on top of the other with the filling in between. In this case serve cut into wedges. Any filling left over can be served like a sauce.

FRUIT CAP PUDDING

Instead of putting the fruit into the sponge it is arranged to top the pudding when it is turned out of the basin. Use the same basic recipe for the sponge as for Sponge Puddings with Dried Fruit (page 68).

Imperial (Metric)	American
Sponge mixture (see page 68)	Sponge mixture (see page 68)
4 to 6 oz (115 to 170g) dried fruit	About 1 cupful dried fruit
Raw cane sugar to taste	Raw cane sugar to taste

1. Soak the fruit overnight in cold water.

2. Add more water and bring to the boil. Simmer for about 30 minutes and sweeten to taste.

3. Make the sponge mixture and grease a pudding basin.

4. Drain the stewed fruit but reserve the liquid. Put the fruit in the bottom of the basin in a thick layer.

5. Spoon in the sponge mixture and steam in the usual way. (See page 16 for notes on steaming.)

6. Steam for 1½ hours then remove wrappers and put a warmed plate on top of the basin. Turn upside down and remove basin.

7. Serve hot with the reserved juice heated to use as a sauce.

Note: For the dried fruit you can use fruit salad, apricots, stoned prunes, peaches or pears. The sponge can be left just plain or flavoured with the finely grated rind of an orange or lemon.

EVE'S PUDDING

If you don't have enough stewed dried fruit to go round put it into a greased pie dish and cover with sponge mixture. Bake as for sponge. Serve hot or cold with real custard or ice-cream. You can use the sponge recipe from Sponge Puddings (page 68) but leave out the dried fruit.

FRUIT CHARLOTTE
Add sultanas (golden seedless raisins) and a few pinches of cinnamon to the filling of an Apple Charlotte.

ROLY POLY
Spread pastry with home-made mincemeat and roll up like a Swiss-roll. Press the ends together to seal and bake as for Spiced Apple Pie (page 76). Makes a quick pudding.

DRIED FRUIT TART
Line a sponge tin with wholemeal pastry and bake blind. When cold fill with a purée of cooked dried fruits. Apricot is particularly good. Fruit should be soaked overnight before cooking for 20 to 30 minutes, then allowed to cool before liquidizing. Sweeten to taste with raw cane sugar.

RICE PUDDING
Add a sprinkle of sultanas (golden seedless raisins) to a rice pudding before baking.

6.

PASTRIES AND PIES

BASIC WHOLEMEAL PASTRY

Imperial (Metric)
½ lb (225g) wholemeal flour
4 oz (115g) polyunsaturated
  margarine
Cold water to mix
More flour for rolling out

American
2 cupsful wholewheat flour
½ cupful polyunsaturated margarine
Cold water to mix
More flour for rolling out

1. Put the flour and margarine into a bowl.

2. Rub in the mixture with the fingers until the mixture resembles fine breadcrumbs.

3. Add about 3 tablespoonsful water and mix to a sticky paste.

4. Add more flour to make one ball of manageable dough that can be rolled out.

Note: Don't knead or work this kind of pastry too much or it will be too tough. It is preferable to add too much water rather than too little — this will avoid dry, tough pastry. The proportion of fat to flour is 1 to 2 so for varying amounts of pastry here is a chart:

Imperial (Metric)	American	Total amount
2 oz (55g) polyunsaturated margarine	¼ cupful	6 oz (170g)
4 oz (115g) flour	1 cupful	
6 oz (170g) polyunsaturated margarine	⅔ cupful	1 lb 2 oz
¾ lb (340g) flour	3 cupsful	
½ lb (225g) polyunsaturated margarine	1 cupful	1½ lb (680g)
1 lb (455g) wholemeal flour	4 cupsful	

Roll out using more wholemeal flour and bake as directed in the recipes that follow in the book. Large pieces, e.g. tops for pies, are best handled by using the rolling pin as a kind of arm to handle the pastry on, rather than trying to move it around with the fingers which will probably tear it. Any small tears or splits can be mended by pressing the pastry firmly together. Joins such as the lid of a pie to the sides should be accomplished by wetting the edge of the bottom part and then pressing the pastry firmly down on to it so that the two pieces stick together. You can use your fingers, the prongs of a fork or the top of a knife blade in a regular pattern to give a professional finish and seal down the lid at the same time.

PIES AND TARTS

Please see page 74 for pastry recipe. Use to make the following selection of pies etc.

SPICED APPLE PIE

A delicious combination of fresh and dried fruit with spice.

Base:

Imperial (Metric)	American
¾ lb (340g) wholemeal pastry	12 ounces wholewheat pastry

Filling:

Imperial (Metric)	American
1½ lbs (680g) cooking apples	1½ pounds cooking apples
¼ level teaspoonful powdered cloves	¼ level teaspoonful powdered cloves
2 heaped tablespoonsful raw cane sugar	2 heaped tablespoonsful raw cane sugar
2 heaped tablespoonsful sultanas	2 heaped tablespoonsful golden seedless raisins
Milk and raw cane sugar for top	Milk and raw cane sugar for top

1. Preheat oven at 400°F/200°C (Gas Mark 6).

2. Line an 8-9 in. (20-23cm) shallow pie dish with two-thirds of the pastry.

3. Peel and core the apples. Slice thinly.

4. Mix the cloves with the sugar and sultanas (golden seedless raisins). Sprinkle the apple slices with this mixture and fill the pie with it.

5. Roll out the remaining one third of the pastry to make a lid. Damp the edge of the pastry around the base and put on the pastry lid. Trim off neatly with a knife and press edges together.

6. Cut a slit in the top to let out the steam. Brush with milk and sprinkle with raw cane sugar.

7. Bake above centre of oven for 20 minutes. Turn down heat to 325°F/170°C (Gas Mark 3) for another 20 minutes to cook the apple.

8. Serve hot from the oven.

Note: As a variation use cinnamon, mixed spice or allspice instead of the cloves, allowing double the amount.

CUSTARD TART

Serves 6 to 8

Base:

Imperial (Metric)
½ lb (225g) wholemeal pastry
   (page 74)

American
8 ounces wholewheat pastry
   (page 74)

Filling:

Imperial (Metric)
3 eggs
1 tablespoonful raw cane sugar
½ pint (285ml) double strength low-
   fat milk*
Few drops pure vanilla flavouring
1 heaped tablespoonful raisins
Nutmeg

American
3 eggs
1 tablespoonful raw cane sugar
1⅓ cupsful double strength low-fat
   milk*
Few drops pure vanilla flavouring
1 heaped tablespoonful raisins
Nutmeg

1. Preheat oven at 400°F/200°C (Gas Mark 6). Place a baking sheet on the centre shelf.

2. Roll out the pastry and line an 8 in. (20cm) quiche dish or tart tin. Trim with a knife and then carefully pull the pastry slightly over the rim with your fingertips. (This will stop the pastry collapsing into the custard.)

3. Break one of the eggs and separate the white from the yolk. Beat the white (in a cup) with a fork and then use it to brush over the pastry base. Sprinkle in the raisins.

4. Whisk the remaining 2 eggs, the egg yolk, sugar and vanilla. Strain through a fine mesh sieve into a jug.

5. Pour gently into the pie shell and sprinkle with a little freshly grated nutmeg.

6. Place carefully (it tends to slop at this stage) on the baking sheet and bake for about 20 minutes.

7. Lower heat to 350°F/180°C (Gas Mark 4) and bake for another 15 to 20 minutes until the custard has set.

* Use dried skimmed milk powder (low-fat). Make up the milk using double the amount of powder suggested on the pack. This will make sure the custard will set and also adds protein.

CHRISTMAS MINCE PIES

Imperial (Metric)
¾ lb (350g) wholemeal pastry (see page 74)
½ tablespoonful brandy
Home-made mincemeat (pages 169-70)

American
12 ounces wholewheat pastry (see page 74)
½ tablespoonful brandy
Home-made mincemeat (pages 169-70)

1. Preheat oven at 400°F/200°C (Gas Mark 6).

2. Roll out pastry thinly.

3. Use a 2½ in. (6cm) round cutter to make 12 bases and a 2 in. (5cm) round cutter to make the tops.

4. Line 12 patty tins with the bases.

5. Mix the brandy with the mincemeat and put 1 teaspoonful (heaped) into each base. Spread flat.

6. Dampen edges and press on the tops. Make a small slit in the top of each one.

7. Bake above centre of the oven for about 15 to 20 minutes.

8. Serve hot or cold.

Note: If you find all mincemeat too rich, add grated apple.

FRUIT SALAD PIE

Imperial (Metric)	American
¾ lb (340g) wholemeal pastry (page 74)	12 ounces wholewheat pastry (page 74)

Filling:

Imperial (Metric)	American
½ lb (225g) dried fruit salad	1½ cupsful dried fruit salad
1 heaped tablespoonful sultanas	1 heaped tablespoonful golden seedless raisins
1 heaped tablespoonful raisins	
Raw cane sugar to taste	1 heaped tablespoonful raisins
½ teaspoonful cinnamon	Raw cane sugar to taste
	½ teaspoonful cinnamon

1. Soak all the fruit overnight in cold water.

2. The next day, bring to the boil and simmer for about 20 minutes. Stir in the sugar and cinnamon.

3. Preheat oven at 450°F/230°C (Gas Mark 7).

4. Line an 8-9 in. (20-23cm) shallow pie dish with two-thirds of the pastry, rolled out thinly.

5. Strain the fruit and reserve the juice.

6. Place the fruit in the lined pie dish. Dampen the edge of the pastry.

7. Roll out the remaining one-third of the pastry and use as a lid. Trim off neatly with a knife and press edges together to seal. Cut a slit in the centre to let out the steam.

8. Bake above centre of oven for 15 minutes then lower the heat to 350°F/180°C (Gas Mark 4) for another 20 minutes to finish cooking the fruit.

9. Serve hot or cold with the reserved juice poured over.

Note: The pie can be brushed with milk and sprinkled with raw cane sugar before baking. My own favourite way of eating dried fruit salad. For special occasions serve with a little single (light) cream or home-made ice cream (vanilla).

Plate Pies

Use a 9 in. (23cm) pie plate which will withstand the heat of the oven. I use an enamel one or an ovenproof glass one. Make the pastry with 6 oz/170g (1½ cupsful) wholemeal (wholewheat) flour and 3 oz/85g (⅓ cupful) polyunsaturated margaine (see page 74).

MINCEMEAT PLATE PIE

Imperial (Metric)
9 oz (255g) wholemeal pastry (page 74)
Home-made mincemeat (pages 169-70)

American
9 ounces wholewheat pastry (page 74)
Home-made mincemeat (pages 169-70

1. Preheat oven at 400°F/200°C (Gas Mark 6).

2. Roll out half the pastry and cover the pie plate.

3. Spread with about 6-7 oz (150-200g) mincemeat, leaving a margin around the edge.

4. Damp the pastry edge with water.

5. Roll out the remaining half of the pastry and cover the pie. Trim edge neatly and press edges together to seal.

6. Cut a few slits in the pastry and bake above centre of the oven for 20 minutes.

7. Lower the heat to 375°F/190°C (Gas Mark 5) and bake for another 15 minutes.

8. Serve hot or cold, cut into wedges.

Note: Makes a popular pudding. If you don't have enough mincemeat add grated apple to make up the amount. Less rich than all mincemeat and cheaper too.

MINTY FRUIT PIE

Make as for Mince Plate Pie but add 5 or 6 fresh mint leaves, finely chopped.

APRICOT PLATE PIE

Make as for Mince Plate Pie but instead of mincemeat use 4 oz/115g (1 cupful) dried apricots. Soak overnight and cook for 20 minutes. Add the finely grated rind of ½ a lemon and a little raw cane sugar to taste.

PEAR PLATE PIE

Make as for Mince Plate Pie but instead of mincemeat use 4 oz/115g (1 cupful) dried pears. Add a few pinches of cinnamon and a little raw cane sugar to taste.

CRUNCHY DATE TART

Use a 9 in (23cm) ovenproof pie plate. Make wholemeal pastry with 4 oz/115g (1 cupful) wholewheat flour and 2 oz/55g (¼ cupful) polyunsaturated margarine.

Base:

Imperial (Metric)	American
6 oz (170g) wholemeal pastry (page 74)	6 ounces wholewheat pastry (page 74)

Filling:

Imperial (Metric)	American
4 oz (115g) chopped, stoned dates	⅔ cupful chopped, stoned dates
About ⅓ pint (200ml) water	¾ cupful water
1½ oz (45g) chopped nuts	2 heaped tablespoonsful chopped nuts

1. Preheat oven at 425°F/220°C (Gas Mark 7).

2. Put the dates into a small saucepan with the water and cook until they form a stiff paste. Leave to cool.

3. Roll out the pastry and line a pie plate. Use your fingers to raise a slight edge all the way round.

4. Spread the date mixture over the pastry.

5. Sprinkle with the nuts, pressing them in lightly.

6. Bake on the top shelf for about 20 minutes.

7. Serve hot or cold.

Variation: Use sunflower seeds instead of the nuts.

STRUDEL
Makes 10 servings

Pastry:

Imperial (Metric)
6 oz (170g) wholemeal flour
1 tablespoonful vegetable oil
1 egg
4 tablespoonsful warm water
Oil for brushing pastry

American
1½ cupsful wholewheat flour
1 tablespoonful vegetable oil
1 egg
4 tablespoonsful warm water
Oil for brushing pastry

Filling:

Imperial (Metric)
1 slice wholemeal bread made into
   crumbs
3 oz (85g) sultanas
2 large cooking apples
2 tablespoonsful raw cane sugar
Juice of 1 small lemon
Rind of 1 small lemon, finely grated
1 teaspoonful cinnamon or mixed
   spice

American
1 slice wholewheat bread made into
   crumbs
½ cupful golden seedless raisins
2 large cooking apples
2 tablespoonsful raw cane sugar
Juice of 1 small lemon
Rind of 1 small lemon, finely grated
1 teapoonful cinnamon or mixed
   spice

1. Put the flour into a bowl and make a well in the centre.

2. Beat the egg in a cup. Add the oil and beat again.

3. Pour into the well in the flour and also add the warm water. Mix together into a wet dough. Knead well until the dough feels smooth.

4. Leave to rest for about 30 minutes then preheat oven at 425°F/220°C (Gas Mark 7).

5. Divide the pastry dough into two pieces. Roll out one half on a large floured sheet of greaseproof paper. Keep rolling it out until it is as thin as paper.

6. Brush with oil, using a pastry brush. Sprinkle with half the breadcrumbs.

7. Put the sultanas (golden seedless raisins) into a bowl. Add the apples, coarsely grated, including the skin. Sprinkle in the sugar, grated rind and juice of the lemon and the spice. Mix well.

8. Use half this filling and spread it over the breadcrumbed pastry. Make sure you leave a margin of ½ in. (1cm) all round for sealing.

9. Wet the margin with cold water and carefully roll up, using the greaseproof paper. This is very easy as once you have started the roll you will only need to keep lifting the greaseproof paper to continue the process. Press the edges to seal where you can, including the ends.

10. Manoeuvre on to a greased baking sheet using the greaseproof paper.

11. Make the other half of the pastry up into a roll and place on the baking sheet. Brush both with oil and bake above centre of the oven for about 40 minutes.

12. Leave on the baking sheet until needed. Cut into pieces with a sharp knife and serve.

Note: Makes a good pudding as well as a snack or pastry for tea. Don't attempt this unless you have both a pastry brush and large sheets of greaseproof paper. It is really quite easy to make as long as you don't try to handle the dough with your fingers, after rolling out.

However don't be afraid to vary the filling with other tart fruits such as strawberries, raspberries or apricots. For the dried fruit you can also use raisins. Use cinnamon with apricots but leave out the spice altogether if using raspberries or strawberries. Cooked, dried apricots can also be used instead of the apple.

FRUIT TURNOVERS

You will need wholemeal pastry (page 74) and a filling from the list below.

1. Preheat oven at 425°F/220°C (Gas Mark 7).

2. Roll out circles of pastry. Dampen the edge all round.

3. Leave a margin around the edge and place filling on one half only.

4. Fold the pastry over the filling and press edges together to seal.

5. Cut a slit in the top half and place on a baking sheet. Bake above centre of the oven for about 15 minutes or until the pastry is cooked.

6. Serve hot or cold.

Fillings:
Use one of the following:

a) Soak dried fruits overnight and cook the following day for about 20 minutes or until tender. Chop into small pieces before using as a filling. Sprinkle with raw cane sugar to taste and a few pinches of cinnamon if you wish. Use apricots, stoned prunes, or dried fruit salad.

b) Thinly sliced apple and a sprinkle of sultanas (golden seedless raisins).

c) Cooked, chopped and stoned prunes with a sprinkle of chopped walnuts (English walnuts).

d) Cooked dried pears and a sprinkle of cinnamon.

e) 1 chopped, cooked fig per turnover with grated cooking apple.

SURPRISE PARCELS

Make miniature turnovers with just one piece of cooked dried fruit inside. Stoned prunes, apricot halves and pieces of peach or pear are ideal. Bake as for turnovers but for less time. These will make a novelty pudding (if you have the time) or are nice to hand round, still warm from the oven, at a party.

7.

BISCUITS, BARS AND COOKIES

FRUIT DIGESTIVES
Makes over 2 dozen biscuits

Imperial (Metric)	American
½ lb (225g) wholemeal flour	2 cupsful wholewheat flour
4 oz (115g) medium oatmeal	1 cupful medium oatmeal
Pinch of powdered cloves	Pinch of powdered cloves
4 oz (115g) polyunsatured margarine	½ cupful polyunsaturated margarine
4 oz (115g) raw cane sugar	⅔ cupful raw cane sugar
1 oz (30g) currants	2 heaped tablespoonsful currants
1 egg, beaten	1 egg, beaten
Milk to mix	Milk to mix

1. Preheat oven at 400°F/200°C (Gas Mark 6).

2. Put the flour, oatmeal and pinch of cloves into a mixing bowl. Mix well.

3. Rub in the margarine until the mixture resembles coarse breadcrumbs.

4. Stir in the sugar and currants.

5. Make a well in the centre and pour in the egg and a little milk. Mix, adding more milk if needed, to a paste.

6. Roll out, using more of the flour, to twice the normal thickness for pastry.

7. Use a tumbler to cut into rounds and place on greased baking sheets. Prick each biscuit with a fork 3 or 4 times.

8. Bake in the centre of the oven for about 15 to 18 minutes.

9. Cool on a wire rack. The digestives will crisp as they cool down so don't overbake. They should still be soft when you take them out of the oven.

10. Store, when cold, in an airtight tin.

Note: A hearty kind of biscuit, high in fibre. Try not to overdo the pinch of powdered cloves as they have a penetrating flavour and will spoil the biscuits if you put in too much.

Variation: Instead of currants use chopped raisins or chopped, stoned dates.

EASTER BISCUITS

Imperial (Metric)
3 oz (85g) polyunsaturated
    margarine
4 oz (115g) raw cane sugar
1 egg
½ lb (225g) wholemeal flour
2 teaspoonsful mixed spice
1 oz (30g) currants

American
⅓ cupful polyunsaturated margarine
⅔ cupful raw cane sugar
1 egg
2 cupsful wholewheat flour
2 teaspoonsful mixed spice
1 heaped tablespoonful currants

1. Preheat oven at 350°F/180°C (Gas Mark 4).

2. Cream the margarine and sugar in a bowl.

3. Beat in the egg and then fold in the flour and spice.

4. Stir in the currants and knead to a firm dough.

5. Roll out to a thickness of ¼ in. (6mm) on a floured worktop. Use shaped cutters to cut into biscuits.

6. Place on a well greased and floured baking sheet and bake near the top of the oven for 18 to 20 minutes.

7. Cool on a wire rack. When cold, store in an airtight container.

FRUIT AND HONEY COOKIES (Basic Recipe)
Makes about 24

For the dried fruit use all one kind or a mixture. Choose from chopped raisins and dates, sultanas (golden seedless raisins), currants, chopped dried bananas, apricots, peaches, pears or de-stoned prunes.

Imperial (Metric)
6 tablespoonsful runny honey
4 oz (115g) polyunsaturated
    margarine
1 egg, beaten
1 oz (30g) ground almonds
6 oz (170g) wholemeal flour
6 oz (170g) dried fruit

American
6 tablespoonsful runny honey
½ cupful polyunsaturated margarine
1 egg, beaten
1½ tablespoonsful ground almonds
1½ cupsful wholewheat flour
1 cupful dried fruit

1. Preheat oven at 375°F/190°C (Gas Mark 5).

2. Put the honey into a mixing bowl with the margarine. Mix/beat until light and creamy.

3. Beat in the egg and ground almonds.

4. Fold in the flour and fruit.

5. Lightly grease baking sheets and use a teaspoon to drop mounds of the mixture on to them, leaving space around each one as they will expand during baking. Flatten them slightly with the back of the spoon.

6. Bake above centre of oven for about 15 minutes.

7. Lift off with a spatula and cool on a wire rack.

8. When cold, store in an airtight container.

FRUIT AND NUT COOKIES

Make as for Fruit and Honey Cookies but use 4 oz/115g (²⁄₃ cupful) dried fruit and 2 oz/55g (¹⁄₃ cupful) chopped nuts.

SPICE AND FRUIT COOKIES

Use the Fruit and Honey Cookies recipe but add ½ teaspoonful mixed spice or cinnamon to the flour.

MUESLI COOKIES

Use the Fruit and Honey Cookies recipe but instead of the dried fruit put in the same weight of home-made muesli (pages 157-59).

FRUIT AND NUT BARS

An extremely chewy substitute for sweets.

Imperial (Metric)	American
3 oz (85g) dates	½ cupful dates
2 oz (55g) figs	⅓ cupful figs
2 oz (55g) raisins	⅓ cupful raisins
3 oz (85g) dried bananas	½ cupful dried bananas
4 oz (115g) dried apricots	. ⅔ cupful dried apricots
2 oz (55g) ground almonds	½ cupful ground almonds
1 oz (30g) polyunsaturated margarine	2½ tablespoonsful polyunsaturated margarine
2 oz (55g) desiccated coconut	⅔ cupful desiccated coconut

1. Chop the dried fruit as small as you can.

2. Melt the margarine very gently, in a saucepan and put in the chopped fruit.

3. Cook very gently until the fruit is soft adding a little water.

4. Put in the almonds and coconut and mix until evenly blended.

5. Put on to a sheet of greaseproof paper and spread out with a palette knife or the back of a spoon.

6. Put another sheet of greaseproof on top and leave to cool and set.

7. Chill in the fridge and cut into fingers or small squares, as required.

Variation: The fruit and nuts can be varied for this recipe. Sultanas (golden seedless raisins), dried papaya, pineapple, etc, but not currants. For the nuts choose from walnuts and hazelnuts. As a substitute for the coconut try chopped sunflower seeds.

DATE TWISTS

Imperial (Metric)	American
½ lb (225g) wholemeal pastry (page 74)	8 ounces wholewheat pastry (page 74)
4 oz (115g) chopped, stoned dates	⅔ cupful chopped, stoned dates
Grated rind and juice of 1 orange	Grated rind and juice of 1 orange
1 heaped tablespoonful chopped nuts	1 heaped tablespoonful chopped nuts
Milk and raw cane sugar for tops	Milk and raw cane sugar for tops

1. Preheat oven at 425°F/220°C (Gas Mark 7).

2. Roll out the pastry to about 12 in. (30cm) square.

3. Put the dates, orange rind and juice into a small pan. Cook the mixture until it has the consistency of jam. Allow to cool.

4. Cut the pastry in half. Spread the filling over one half. Place the other half of the pastry on top, like a sandwich.

5. Use a knife to cut into oblongs. Make 3 rows across the narrowest width and then cut across the sandwich 5 times lengthways. This will give you 18 pieces.

6. Twist each one in the centre so that they form a bow shape and place on an ungreased baking sheet.

7. Brush with a little milk and sprinkle with sugar.

8. Bake for 12 to 15 minutes near the top of the oven.

9. Eat freshly baked, preferably still warm from the oven.

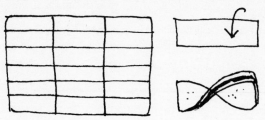

APRICOT FINGERS
Makes about 18

Imperial (Metric)
½ lb (225g) wholemeal flour
1 level teaspoonful baking powder
4 oz (115g) polyunsaturated
  margarine
2 oz (55g) raw cane sugar
1 egg, beaten

American
2 cupsful wholewheat flour
1 level teaspoonful baking powder
½ cupful polyunsaturated margarine
⅓ cupful raw cane sugar
1 egg, beaten

Filling:

Imperial (Metric)
½ lb (225g) dried apricots, soaked
  and cooked
1 heaped tablespoonful raw cane
  sugar
½ level teaspoonful cinnamon
1 heaped tablespoonful sultanas

American
1⅓ cupsful dried apricots, soaked
  and cooked
1 heaped tablespoonful raw cane
  sugar
½ level teaspoonful cinnamon
1 heaped tablespoonful golden
  seedless raisins

1. Preheat oven at 350°F/180°C (Gas Mark 4).

2. Put the flour into a bowl and sprinkle in the baking powder.

3. Rub in the margarine until the mixture resembles fine breadcrumbs.

4. Stir in the sugar and egg. Mix to a dough and knead lightly.

5. Roll out half the dough and line an 8 × 11 in. (20 × 28cm) baking tin to make a base.

6. Chop the cooled apricots with a little of their juice and mix with the remaining filling ingredients. Spread over the base.

7. Roll out the rest of the pastry dough to make a cover for the filling. (This will have to be trimmed straight before you put it on.)

8. Bake on the centre shelf for about 1 hour.

9. Take out of the oven and leave to cool in the tin. Cut into fingers and remove from the tin.

Note: Eat on the day they are baked and serve for a pudding, snack or for tea.

GARIBALDI BISCUITS

Use up any left-over raw pastry to make these. Roll out the pastry and cut in half. Sprinkle one half with currants and a little raw cane sugar, after first brushing with milk. Place the other half on top and press together lightly with the rolling pin. Cut into fingers and bake in a preheated oven at 400°F/200°C (Gas Mark 6) on the top shelf for about 15 minutes.

FIG ROLLS

Make 'sausage rolls' with left-over pastry and a filling of cooked, mashed figs. Cut slits along the top, diagonally and bake as for Garibaldi biscuits.

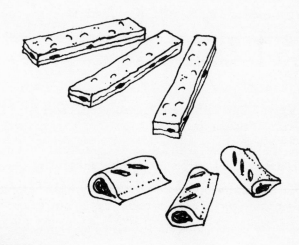

DATE SLICES
Makes 20

Filling:

Imperial (Metric)	American
1 tablespoonful honey	1 tablespoonful honey
Juice of ½ a lemon	Juice of ½ a lemon
3 tablespoonsful water	3 tablespoonsful water
6 oz (170g) chopped, stoned dates	1 cupful chopped, stoned dates

Base:

Imperial (Metric)	American
½ lb (225g) wholemeal flour	2 cupsful wholewheat flour
4 oz (115g) rolled oats	1 cupful rolled oats
6 oz (170g) polyunsaturated margarine	¾ cupful polyunsaturated margarine
2 oz (55g) raw cane sugar	⅓ cupful raw cane sugar

1. Put the ingredients for the filling into a small saucepan. Heat and simmer while you stir until the dates have softened. (Add more water if it goes too dry.)

2. Preheat oven at 375°F/190°C (Gas Mark 5).

3. Put the flour and oats into a mixing bowl and mix well.

4. Add the margarine and rub in with the fingers.

5. Stir in the sugar.

6. Grease and line with greased greaseproof paper a 7×11 in. (17×27cm) baking tray.

7. Cover the base evenly with half the flour mixture. Press it down well so that it will not be too crumbly after baking.

8. Spread the fruit mixture over this base and sprinkle the remaining flour mixture over the top as evenly as you can. Press firmly.

9. Bake above centre of oven for about 35 to 40 minutes.

10. Allow to cool a little then cut into slices (about 20).

11. Leave in the tin to grow cold and remove carefully to store in an airtight container.

Note: A high-fibre recipe. The fruit can be varied — dried apricots, destoned prunes, figs or a mixture. (Some people may prefer a filling that is not as sweet as dates.)

8.

CAKES

BASIC FRUIT CAKE

This is a quickly made cake in which the fruit and flavouring can be varied according to what is in the storecupboard. A good staple that bridges the gap between a tea bread and a rich fruit cake. A plainish, semi-sweet cake.

Imperial (Metric)
½ lb (225g) wholemeal flour
2 level teaspoonsful baking powder
1 level teaspoonful cinnamon
1 level teaspoonful mixed spice
3 oz (85g) polyunsaturated margarine
3 oz (75g) raw cane sugar
4 oz (115g) sultanas
4 oz (115g) currants
Grated rind of 1 lemon
1 egg
Milk to mix

American
2 cupsful wholewheat flour
2 level teaspoonsful baking powder
1 level teaspoonful cinnamon
1 level teaspoonful mixed spice
⅓ cupful polyunsaturated margarine
½ cupful raw cane sugar
⅔ cupful golden seedless raisins
⅔ cupful currants
Grated rind of 1 lemon
1 egg
Milk to mix

1. Preheat oven at 350°F/180°C (Gas Mark 4).

2. Put the flour into a bowl with the baking powder and spices. Mix well.

3. Rub in the margarine until the mixture resembles breadcrumbs.

4. Stir in the sugar, dried fruit and rind.

5. Beat the egg, in a cup, and add to the bowl. Stir in with enough milk to make a soft dropping consistency, i.e. so that it will drop off the spoon easily.

6. Grease and flour a 2 lb (1kg) loaf tin. Turn the mixture into this and bake in the centre of the oven for about 1 hour to 1 hour and 10 minutes.

7. Take out of the oven and let the sides shrink away from the tin before turning out on a wire rack to cool. If you are not sure that it is done, test with a skewer. If it comes out clean, then the cake is done.

8. Serve in thickly cut slices.

Note: The fruit can be varied in the following ways:

a) Use all sultanas (golden seedless raisins) or all raisins.

b) Use chopped, stoned dates or dried apricots.

c) Use chopped, dried bananas and pineapple.

Whatever combination of fruit you use the total weight should be in the region of ½ lb/225g (1⅓ cupsful).

EGGLESS FRUIT CAKE

The vinegar in this recipe is used as a raising agent and its taste is undetectable in the finished cake.

Imperial (Metric)	American
½ lb (225g) wholemeal flour	2 cupsful wholewheat flour
1 teaspoonful bicarbonate of soda	1 teaspoonful baking soda
4 oz (115g) polyunsaturated margarine	½ cupful polyunsaturated margarine
¼ pint (170ml) milk	⅔ cupful milk
1 tablespoonful black treacle	1 tablespoonful molasses
3 oz (85g) raw cane sugar	½ cupful raw cane sugar
4 oz (115g) dried fruit	⅔ cupful dried fruit
2 oz (55g) chopped walnuts	⅓ cupful chopped English walnuts
2 tablespoonsful wine vinegar	2 tablespoonsful wine vinegar

1. Preheat oven at 325°F/170°C (Gas Mark 3).

2. Mix the flour and bicarbonate of soda (baking soda) in a mixing bowl.

3. Add the margarine and rub in with the fingers until the mixture resembles breadcrumbs.

4. Make a well in the centre and pour in the milk, with the black treacle (molasses), sugar, dried fruit and nuts. Fold together, using a metal spoon until lightly blended.

5. Lastly fold in the vinegar. It is important not to beat the mixture.

6. Turn into a greased and lined 6 in. (15cm) diameter cake tin.

7. Bake above centre of oven for up to 1½ hours, testing with a skewer to see if it is cooked after 1¼ hours.

8. Cool in the tin for 5 minutes, then turn out on to a wire rack to grow cold, after removing lining paper.

Variation: Use all dried fruit instead of a combination of fruit and nuts. For the fruit a mixture is best — currants, raisins, sultanas (golden seedless raisins), chopped dried apricots.

HONEY CAKE WITH FRUIT AND NUTS

An old fashioned sort of cake that keeps well.

Imperial (Metric)
½ lb (225g) wholemeal flour
3 level teaspoonsful baking powder
4 oz (115g) polyunsaturated
  margarine
4 oz (115g) dried fruit (see list
  below)
2 tablespoonsful runny honey
2 eggs, beaten
1 oz (30g) chopped nuts
4 tablespoonsful milk

American
2 cupsful wholewheat flour
3 level teaspoonsful baking powder
½ cupful polyunsaturated margarine
⅔ cupful dried fruit (see list below)
2 tablespoonsful runny honey
2 eggs, beaten
1 heaped tablespoonful chopped
  nuts
4 tablespoonsful milk

1. Preheat oven at 350°F/180°C (Gas Mark 4).

2. Put the flour and baking powder into a bowl and mix well.

3. Rub in the margarine until the mixture resembles fine breadcrumbs.

4. Add the dried fruit, honey, eggs, nuts and milk. Mix well.

5. Pour into a greased 7 in. (18cm) square tin.

6. Bake above centre of oven for about 1 hour and 10 minutes. When the cake is done it should feel firm and springy to the touch.

7. Allow to shrink away from the sides of the tin for a few minutes, then turn out on to a wire rack to cool.

Note: For the fruit and nuts use one of the following combinations:

a) Stoned, sliced dates with walnuts (English walnuts).

b) Chopped, dried apricots with almonds.

c) Chopped, stoned prunes with walnuts (English walnuts).

d) Raisins and walnuts (English walnuts).

CARROT CAKE

A high-fibre cake with a moist texture. Eat within two days of baking. If the carrot is very sweet, cut back on the sugar a little.

Imperial (Metric)	American
¼ pint (140ml) water	⅔ cupful water
6 oz (170g) dried fruit*	1 cupful dried fruit*
4 oz (115g) polyunsaturated margarine	½ cupful polyunsaturated margarine
6 oz (170g) fresh carrot, grated finely	1 cupful finely grated fresh carrot
4 oz (115g) raw cane sugar	⅔ cupful raw cane sugar
5 tablespoonsful runny honey	5 tablespoonsful runny honey
4 pinches ground nutmeg	4 pinches ground nutmeg
1 egg	1 egg
½ lb (225g) wholemeal flour	2 cupsful wholewheat flour
2 level teaspoonsful baking powder	2 level teaspoonsful baking soda

1. Put the first 7 ingredients into a saucepan. Bring slowly to the boil while you stir and simmer for 5 to 6 minutes.

2. Spoon into a mixing bowl and leave to grow cold.

3. Preheat oven at 350°F/180°C (Gas Mark 4).

4. Beat the egg and stir into the cooled mixture.

5. Grease and flour a 9 in. (23cm) round cake tin.

6. Sprinkle the flour and baking powder into the mixture and stir well.

7. Turn into the prepared cake tin and bake above centre of oven for up to an hour. Test to see if the cake is done by pressing with the fingers. The cake should feel firm and spring back into shape.

8. Take out of the tin and cool on a wire rack.

* For the fruit use a mixture of two or more of the following to make up the weight given:
Sultanas (golden seedless raisins)

Seedless raisins
Chopped, stoned dates
Chopped, stoned prunes

CHEQUERS CAKE

A very attractive topping and a semi-sweet base make this an interesting cake or pudding.

Imperial (Metric)	American
13 dried apricots	13 dried apricots
12 pitted prunes	12 pitted prunes
¼ teaspoonful cinnamon	¼ teaspoonful ground cinnamon
1 oz (30g) butter	2½ tablespoonsful butter

Cake:

Imperial (Metric)	American
½ lb (225g) wholemeal flour	2 cupsful wholewheat flour
1 teaspoonful baking powder	1 teaspoonful baking powder
4 oz (115g) polyunsaturated margarine	½ cupful polyunsaturated margarine
4 oz (115g) raw cane sugar	⅔ cupful raw cane sugar
6 tablespoonsful milk	6 tablespoonsful milk

1. Put the fruit into a small saucepan and cover with boiling water. Leave to soak for about 2 hours.

2. Bring to the boil and simmer for about 15 minutes. Drain well and put aside for the topping.

3. Preheat oven at 375°F/190°C (Gas Mark 5).

4. Melt the butter in a small saucepan. Sprinkle in the cinnamon and set aside for the topping.

5. Mix the flour and baking powder in a bowl.

6. Rub in the margarine with the fingers until the mixture resembles breadcrumbs.

7. Stir in the sugar and spoon in the milk. Mix to a soft paste.

8. Turn into a greased and lined 8 in. (20cm) square cake tin and flatten with a knife.

9. Lightly press in the fruit in an alternating pattern, starting with an apricot in each corner, as shown.

10. Brush with the butter mixture and bake on the centre shelf for about 40 to 45 minutes.

11. Cool in the tin for about 3 minutes then lift out. Remove paper and serve. Cut into neat squares and serve with single (light) cream or ice-cream.

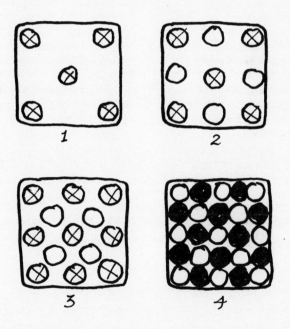

GUGELHOPF

This Austrian cake is baked in a decoratively patterned mould with a centre tube. Traditionally this kind of cake is dusted with icing (confectioner's) sugar. True wholefooders will faint at the thought of icing sugar and will have to make do with a scattering of chopped nuts. A remarkably light, semi-sweet cake. This recipe is for a 6 in. (15cm) diameter mould, available from good kitchen shops.

Imperial (Metric)	American
2 oz (55g) dried fruit*	1/3 cupful dried fruit*
1/2 oz (15g) fresh yeast or 1/4 oz (7g) 'instant' yeast	1 tablespoonful fresh yeast or 1/2 tablespoonful 'instant' yeast
5 tablespoonsful warm milk	5 tablespoonsful warm milk
6 oz (150g) wholemeal flour	11/2 cupsful wholewheat flour
2 oz (55g) polyunsaturated margarine	1/4 cupful polyunsaturated margarine
1 egg, beaten	1 egg, beaten
2 oz (55g) raw cane sugar	1/3 cupful raw cane sugar
Rind of 1 orange, finely grated	Rind of 1 orange, finely grated
Juice of 1 orange	Juice of 1 orange
10 shelled almonds, chopped	10 shelled almonds, chopped

1. Put the dried fruit of your choice into a basin and pour over boiling water, enough to cover. Leave to soak for about an hour.

2. Crumble the yeast into a cup and mix to a cream with a tablespoonful of the warm milk. Add the rest of the warm milk and mix well. Add a tablespoonful of the flour and mix again. Leave to rise in a warm place.

3. Gently melt the margarine and leave to cool a little.

4. Put the yeast mixture into a mixing bowl and, one at a time, beat in the melted margarine, sugar, beaten egg, orange juice and rind and lastly the dried fruit.

5. Finally beat in the flour a little at a time to make a very soft dough rather like a cake mixture.

6. Preheat oven at 375°F/190°C (Gas Mark 5).

7. Paint the inside of the mould with oil, making sure all the surface is covered, including the funnel. (Use a pastry brush.)

8. Scatter in the chopped almonds and turn in the dough which should half fill the mould.

9. Leave to rise in a warm place until the dough reaches the top of the mould.

10. Bake on a shelf above centre for about 35 minutes. Turn out of the mould and cool on a wire rack. Eat freshly baked for a snack or tea.

* Chopped dried apricots, raisins, sultanas (golden seedless raisins) and chopped dried peaches are all suitable. For variation use the juice and rind of a lemon and chopped, de-stoned prunes.

Note: If using 'instant' yeast then ignore stage 2. Instead, mix the instant yeast dry into the flour and put in the milk, melted margarine, sugar, beaten egg, orange juice, rind and dried fruit. Mix to a soft dough and follow recipe instruction from point 6.

GÂTEAU NORMANDE

Makes 8 generous slices

Whisked Sponge:

Imperial (Metric)
3 eggs
4½ oz (130g) raw cane sugar
3 oz (85g) wholemeal flour
1 teaspoonful mixed spice or
    cinnamon

American
3 eggs
Generous ⅔ cupful raw cane sugar
¾ cupful wholewheat flour
1 teaspoonful mixed spice or
    cinnamon

Filling:

Imperial (Metric)
1 lb (455g) cooking apples
2 tablespoonsful raw sugar jam
2 oz (55g) sultanas
2 oz (55g) raisins
1 tablespoonful raw cane sugar
⅓ pint (200ml) double cream,
    whipped

American
1 pound cooking apples
2 tablespoonsful raw sugar jelly
⅓ cupful raisins
⅓ cupful golden seedless raisins
1 tablespoonful raw cane sugar
1 cupful heavy cream, whipped

1. Preheat oven at 375°F/190°C (Gas Mark 5).

2. Grease and line with greased, greaseproof paper an 8 in. (20cm) square or a 9 in. (23cm) round sponge tin, depending on which shape you want your gâteau to be.

3. Whisk the eggs with the sugar until thick — rather like a mousse texture — with an electric beater. (If you don't have an electric beater they must be whisked by hand over a pan of hot water, which takes much longer.)

4. Fold in the flour with a metal spoon, via a metal fine mesh sieve. Add the bran, which will be left in the sieve, and fold that in too. Add the spice. Mix well.

5. Pour into the prepared tin and bake above centre of oven for about 35 minutes. When the cake is done it will feel springy if you press the top lightly with your fingers.

6. Take out of the tin and cool on a wire rack.

7. Peel and core the apples. Slice thinly (or grate coarsely) and put into a saucepan with the jam. Put the lid on and cook very gently until soft.

8. Stir in the dried fruit and sugar and leave to grow cold.

9. Remove the greaseproof paper from the sponge and split in half with a sharp knife.

10. Spread both halves with the cream.

11. Spoon the filling over the bottom half and carefully sandwich the two halves together.

12. Serve freshly made.

Variation: Use honey instead of the jam for the filling.

Note: Although this recipe has much less fat than the usual type of gâteau, it is still high in calories.

CHRISTMAS CAKE

A very rich, dark fruit cake that is also suitable for wedding, christening and birthday cakes. Amounts shown are for an 8 in. (20cm) square, or, 9 in. (23cm) round, cake. '

As there are 18 ingredients in this recipe I have divided them into 4 groups to make things a little easier.

Group A:

Imperial (Metric)	American
¾ lb (340g) wholemeal flour	3 cupsful wholewheat flour
2 teaspoonsful mixed spice	2 teaspoonsful mixed spice
2 teaspoonsful cinnamon	2 teaspoonsful cinnamon
¼ teaspoonsful sea salt	¼ teaspoonful sea salt
4 oz (115g) ground almonds	¾ cupful ground almonds

Group B:

Imperial (Metric)	American
4 eggs	4 eggs
4 tablespoonsful sherry or brandy	4 tablespoonsful sherry or brandy
2 tablespoonsful milk	2 tablespoonsful milk

Group C:

Imperial (Metric)	American
½ lb (225g) polyunsaturated margarine	1 cupful polyunsaturated margarine
½ lb (225g) raw cane sugar	1⅓ cupsful raw cane sugar
1 generous tablespoonful black treacle	1 generous tablespoonful molasses

Group D:

Imperial (Metric)	American
Grated rind of 1 lemon	Grated rind of 1 lemon
Grated rind of 2 oranges	Grated rind of 2 oranges
6 oz (170g) dried apricots	1 cupful chopped, dried apricots

1 lb (455g) currants	2½ cupsful currants
½ lb (225g) seedless raisins	1⅓ cupsful seedless raisins
½ lb (225g) sultanas	1⅓ cupsful golden seedless raisins
2 oz (55g) chopped, pitted prunes	⅓ cupful chopped, pitted prunes

1. Mix all the ingredients in group A, using a large mixing bowl.

2. Preheat oven at 325°F/170°C (Gas Mark 3).

3. Prepare the cake tin. Grease, then line with a double thickness of greased greaseproof paper. Tie a double band of brown paper around the outside of the tin, using a type of string that will withstand the heat of the oven. The paper must extend beyond the top of the tin.

4. Now use the ingredients in group B. Whisk the eggs in a basin. Add the alcohol and milk and whisk again. Put to one side.

5. Use group C. In a large mixing bowl cream the margarine, sugar and black treacle. Beat until soft.

6. Gradually stir in the flour and egg mixtures you have already prepared, adding them alternately.

7. Last of all, stir in group D. Stir well until evenly distributed.

8. Spoon into the prepared tin and flatten with a knife. If you want the top of the cake to be level after baking, make a slight well in the centre of the cake. As this will rise more than the outside it should turn out reasonably flat.

9. Bake on the middle shelf for 1½ hours, turning down the heat to 300°F/150°C (Gas Mark 2) for another 1¾ to 2 hours. (Total baking time will be about 3¼ to 3½ hours so make sure you don't need your oven for anything else during such a long period.) If the top begins to get too dark, cover with a double sheet of greaseproof paper.

10. Cool in the tin, overnight. When absolutely cold, store in an airtight tin.

continued overleaf.

Make this cake in November, or even earlier, and let everyone know Christmas is coming. After storing for a week, open the tin, prick the top of the cake with a fork and dribble in a little sherry. Put the lid back on and leave to mature. Add a little more sherry every ten days or so until it is time to use the cake. This will ensure the cake is nice and moist when cut.

A good Christmas cake should cut cleanly, be moist, rich and dark. A wholefood cake should not contain glacé cherries or candied peel, or be iced with white icing. (It should also not be made with white flour or sugar.) So how are you going to decorate it? I suggest marzipan made with raw cane sugar on the top, decorated with an assortment of halved, shelled nuts, arranged in a pattern and pressed slightly into the surface of the marzipan. Leave room for any traditional decorations such as holly, etc. The marzipan can be attached to the cake with a thin spread of raw sugar jam (jelly). Cover the sides with a suitable cake frill.

BOILED FRUIT CAKE
A heavy fruit cake that keeps well, with the novelty of being made partly in a saucepan — hence its name.

Imperial (Metric)	American
5 oz (140g) polyunsaturated margarine	Generous ½ cupful polyunsaturated margarine
6 oz (170g) black treacle	6 tablespoonsful molasses
½ lb (225g) raisins	1⅓ cupsful raisins
½ lb (225g) currants	1⅓ cupsful currants
4 oz (115g) sultanas	⅔ cupful golden seedless raisins
4 oz (115g) stoned, chopped dates	⅔ cupful stoned, chopped dates
4 oz (115g) chopped, dried apricots	⅔ cupful chopped, dried apricots
6 fl oz (170ml) milk	¾ cupful milk
Grated rinds of 1 lemon and 1 orange	Grated rinds of 1 lemon and 1 orange
2 eggs, beaten	2 eggs, beaten
1 heaped teaspoonful mixed spice	1 heaped teaspoonful mixed spice
½ teaspoonful grated nutmeg	½ teaspoonful grated nutmeg
½ lb (225g) wholemeal flour	2 cupsful wholewheat flour
½ level teaspoonful bicarbonate of soda	½ slightly heaped teaspoonful baking soda

1. Preheat oven at 300°F/150°C (Gas Mark 2).

2. Grease a 7 in. (18cm) round cake tin and line with greased greaseproof paper.

3. Put the margarine, black treacle (molasses), dried fruit, milk and rinds into a saucepan.

4. Heat gently until the margarine has melted then simmer while you stir for about 4 or 5 minutes.

5. Take off the heat and cool to lukewarm.

6. Put the spices and flour into a bowl and mix.

7. Add the beaten eggs but don't stir yet.

8. Sprinkle the bicarbonate of soda into the saucepan with the cooled fruit mixture and stir.

9. Quickly mix into the flour/eggs and beat well.

10. Spoon into prepared tin and bake for about 1 hour 50 minutes to 2 hours.

11. Turn out of tin on to wire rack.

12. Allow to grow cold and wrap in greaseproof paper before storing in an airtight container.

WHOLEFOOD DUNDEE CAKE

Based on a traditional recipe from Scotland, this cake keeps well and has a lot of personality. It is not as rich as the heavier type of fruit cake and is a good traveller — ideal for packed lunches and picnics. Chopped dried apricots are used instead of glacé cherries and fresh orange and lemon rind instead of candied peel as in ordinary Dundee Cake recipes.

Imperial (Metric)	American
6 oz (170g) raw cane sugar	1 cupful raw cane sugar
5 oz (140g) polyunsaturated margarine	Generous ½ cupful polyunsaturated margarine
½ lb (225g) wholemeal flour	2 cupsful wholewheat flour
1 heaped teaspoonful baking powder	2 level teaspoonsful baking powder
2 level teaspoonsful mixed spice	2 level teaspoonsful mixed spice
3 eggs, beaten	3 eggs, beaten
Milk to mix	Milk to mix
5 oz (140g) each of:	1 cupful each of:
currants	currants
sultanas	golden seedless raisins
seedless raisins	seedless raisins
chopped dried apricots	chopped dried apricots
Grated rind of 1 lemon and 1 orange	Grated rind of 1 lemon and 1 orange
2 oz (55g) chopped almonds	½ cupful chopped almonds
Split almonds for decoration	Split almonds for decoration

1. Preheat oven at 350°F/180°C (Gas Mark 4).

2. Put sugar, margarine, flour, baking powder (baking soda) and spice into a bowl with the eggs. Mix, then beat with enough milk to a consistency that will drop slowly off the spoon. (If too soft it will not hold up the fruit and if too stiff the cake will be dry.)

3. Stir in the fruit, rind and chopped almonds.

4. Spoon into a well-greased and floured cake tin, 8 in. (20cm) diameter. Flatten with a knife then make a slight hollow in the middle.

5. Decorate with the split almonds, laying them in circles, starting with the outside edge.

6. Bake on the middle shelf for about 2 hours. The heat can be turned down slightly after 1½ hours.

7. Cool in the tin for several minutes then turn out on to a wire rack to grow cold. Store in an airtight tin.

8. Keep for a few days before cutting.

FRUIT SALAD CAKE

This cake has a more delicate taste than ordinary fruit cake and the pale colours of the apricots, pears and apple contrast with the dark brown of the prunes.

Imperial (Metric)	American
4 oz (115g) raw cane sugar	⅔ cupful raw cane sugar
4 oz (115g) polyunsaturated margarine	½ cupful polyunsaturated margarine
1 tablespoonful liquid honey	1 tablespoonful liquid honey
2 eggs	2 eggs
½ lb (225g) wholemeal flour	2 cupsful wholewheat flour
2 level teaspoonsful baking powder	2 level teaspoonsful baking powder
1 teaspoonful cinnamon	1 teaspoonful cinnamon
Milk to mix	Milk to mix
½ lb (225g) chopped dried fruit salad*	1½ cupsful chopped dried fruit salad*
Grated rind of 1 lemon	Grated rind of 1 lemon

1. Preheat oven at 350°F/180°C (Gas Mark 4).

2. Mix the sugar, honey, margarine, eggs, flour, baking powder and cinnamon.

3. Add enough milk to make a soft consistency and beat well. The mixture should drop slowly off the spoon.

4. Stir in (don't beat) the chopped fruit and rind.

5. Turn into a well-greased and floured 7 in. (18cm) diameter cake tin and flatten with a knife.

6. Bake on the middle shelf for just over 1¼ hours.

7. Cool in the tin for a few minutes, then turn out on to a wire rack to cool.

8. Store in an airtight tin.

Variation: The top of the cake can be sprinkled with flaked almonds before baking to give it an attractive finish.

* De-stone prunes before weighing. A ½ pound (225g) pack of dried fruit salad will give you enough fruit after de-stoning. Chop the fruit as small as raisins.

ECCLES CAKES
Makes about 16

Imperial (Metric)	American
Approx. 10 oz (285g) wholemeal pastry (page 74)	Approx. 10 ounces wholewheat pastry (page 74)

Filling:

Imperial (Metric)	American
1 oz (30g) polyunsaturated margarine	2½ tablespoonsful polyunsaturated margarine
½ teaspoonful mixed spice	½ teaspoonful mixed spice
Grated rind of 1 lemon	Grated rind of 1 lemon
4 oz (115g) currants	½ cupful currants
1 apple, coarsely grated	1 apple, coarsely grated
1 tablespoonful raw cane sugar	1 tablespoonful raw cane sugar
Melted honey for glaze	Melted honey for glaze

1. Preheat oven at 425°F/220°C (Gas Mark 7).

2. Roll out pastry to ⅛ in. thick (3mm) and cut into about 15 or 16 rounds.

3. Take each circle and lightly roll with the rolling pin to make them larger and thinner.

4. Melt the margarine in a small saucepan. Add the remaining ingredients for the filling and mix well.

5. Take a pastry circle and brush all round the edge with water.

6. Put a heaped teaspoonful of the filling in the middle.

7. Gather the edges of the pastry together, using your fingertips, and seal them together. You should now have a little 'purse' with the filling completely enclosed.

8. Turn upside down on to a baking sheet and flatten very gently. This needs to be done carefully so as not to burst it.

9. Use a sharp knife to make slits across the top. Repeat for the remaining Eccles Cakes.

10. Bake above centre of oven for about 20 to 25 minutes.

11. Glaze with melted honey and leave to cool on a wire rack.

12. Eat freshly baked.

Note: Served hot from the oven with real egg custard these will make a good pudding. This recipe is a wholefood version of the traditional British cake, although nowadays 'pastry' would seem to be a more apt description.

QUEEN CAKES
Makes 24

Very dainty cakes with a delicate flavour. Twenty-four sounds a lot but as they are small they soon disappear. At adventurous kitchen shops you can buy fluted patty tins specially for these little cakes.

Imperial (Metric)	American
½ lb (225g) wholemeal flour	2 cupsful wholewheat flour
1½ level teaspoonsful baking powder	1½ level teaspoonsful baking powder
4 oz (115g) polyunsaturated margarine	½ cupful polyunsaturated margarine
4 oz (115g) raw cane sugar	⅔ cupful raw cane sugar
3 tablespoonsful top of the milk or single cream	3 tablespoonsful top of the milk or light cream
1 egg, beaten	1 egg, beaten
4 oz (115g) currants	⅔ cupful currants
Grated rind ½ lemon	Grated rind ½ lemon
Milk	Milk

1. Preheat oven at 400°F/200°C (Gas Mark 6).

2. Put the flour and baking powder into a bowl and mix well.

3. In a separate bowl, cream the margarine, sugar and top of the milk (or cream).

4. Gradually add the egg and flour plus the baking powder. Mix well.

5. Put in the currants, lemon rind and enough milk to make a thick batter.

6. Grease 24 patty tins and spoon the mixture into the moulds. Don't fill them too full or the shape of the cakes will be spoiled.

7. Bake for about 25 minutes above the centre of the oven.

8. Serve still warm from the oven for tea or for a snack.

ROCK CAKES

The secret of success with these quickly made cakes is not to overbake them which will ensure they stay moist and don't dry out too much during baking. Use a knife to mix them.

Imperial (Metric)	American
6 oz (170g) wholemeal flour	1½ cupsful wholewheat flour
1 level teaspoonful baking powder	1 level teaspoonful baking powder
¼ teaspoonful grated nutmeg	¼ teaspoonful grated nutmeg
¼ teaspoonful mixed spice	¼ teaspoonful mixed spice
2½ oz (70g) polyunsaturated margarine	Approx. ⅓ cupful polyunsaturated margarine
3 oz (85g) raw cane sugar	½ cupful raw cane sugar
3 oz (85g) currants	½ cupful currants
2 oz (55g) sultanas	⅓ cupful golden seedless raisins
Grated rind of an orange *or* lemon	Grated rind of an orange *or* lemon
1 egg, beaten	1 egg, beaten
Milk to mix	Milk to mix

1. Preheat oven at 375°F/190°C (Gas Mark 5).

2. Grease and flour a baking sheet.

3. Put the flour, baking powder, nutmeg and mixed spice into a bowl. Mix.

4. Add the margarine and rub in with the fingertips until the mixture resembles fine breadcrumbs.

5. Sprinkle in the sugar, dried fruit and grated rind. Mix again.

6. Stir in the beaten egg and enough milk to make a stiff mixture.

7. Spoon into heaps on the prepared baking sheet, leaving enough room for them to spread during baking. Sprinkle with a little more sugar to make a crisp top on each one if you wish.

8. Bake above centre of oven for about 15 to 20 minutes.

9. Eat warm from the oven for a snack or for tea.

APRICOT NUBBIES

Make and bake as for Rock Cakes but use chopped apricots for the dried fruit and cinnamon for the spice.

QUICK FRUIT BUNS

Imperial (Metric)	American
4 oz (115g) wholemeal flour	1 cupful wholewheat flour
1 level teaspoonful baking powder	1 teaspoonful baking powder
4 oz (115g) polyunsaturated margarine	½ cupful polyunsaturated margarine
4 oz (100g) raw cane sugar	⅔ cupful raw cane sugar
2 eggs	2 eggs
2 oz (55g) dried fruit	⅓ cupful dried fruit

1. Preheat oven at 375°F/190°C (Gas Mark 5).

2. Put the flour, baking powder, margarine, sugar and eggs into a bowl. Mix and beat to a smooth cake mix.

3. Stir in the dried fruit of your choice.

4. Spoon into about 14 or 15 small paper cases arranged in patty tins.

5. Bake on the centre shelf and above centre for about 20 minutes.

6. Cool on a wire rack.

For the fruit use currants, or sultanas (golden seedless raisins), or raisins, or chopped dried bananas, dates, apricots, peaches, pears or pineapple. Grated orange or lemon rind can also be used for extra flavour, also carob powder, ginger, spices and pure vanilla flavouring. Here are some combinations:

a) Currants and lemon rind.

b) Raisins and orange rind.

c) Currants, sultanas (golden seedless raisins) and raisins mixed and ½ teaspoonful mixed spice or cinnamon.

d) Lemon rind and dried bananas or apricots.

e) Dried pears and ½ teaspoonful cinnamon.

f) Peaches and a few drops of pure vanilla flavouring.

g) ½ teaspoonful ground ginger and chopped dates.

h) 1 tablespoonful carob powder and pineapple.

Note: It would be difficult to find a recipe that can be made up more quickly than this one, or one that is more versatile. Make them in emergencies and serve still warm from the oven.

APPLE AND SULTANA SPICE CAKE

Makes 16 large squares

Imperial (Metric)
4 oz (115g) polyunsaturated
  margarine
10 oz (285g) wholemeal flour
2 level teaspoonsful baking powder
3 oz (85g) sultanas
½ lb (225g) raw cane sugar
1½ teaspoonsful cinnamon
2 eggs, beaten
6 fl oz (170ml) milk
½ lb (225g) coarsely grated apple
  (leave the skin on)

American
½ cupful polyunsaturated margarine
2½ cupsful wholewheat flour
2 level teaspoonsful baking powder
½ cupful golden seedless raisins
1⅓ cupsful raw cane sugar
1 teaspoonful ground cinnamon
2 eggs, beaten
⅔ cupful milk
1⅓ cupful coarsely grated apple
  (leave the skin on)

1. Preheat oven at 350°F/180°C (Gas Mark 4).

2. Grease and line with greased greaseproof paper, an 8 in. (20cm) square cake tin.

3. Melt the margarine in a small saucepan. Allow to cool.

4. Put the flour, baking powder, sultanas (golden seedless raisins), sugar and spice into a large mixing bowl. Mix well.

5. Stir in the melted margarine, the beaten eggs, milk and grated apple. Beat to a smooth, thick batter.

6. Turn into the prepared tin and bake on the middle shelf of the oven for an hour or a little longer. When it is cooked the cake will spring back if you press it lightly with your fingers.

7. Turn out on to a wire rack to cool and remove greaseproof paper.

8. Serve for a sweet, for tea, elevenses or a snack.

Note: An extremely filling, family cake that is quick to prepare. Eat within 2 days of baking. Very similar in taste and texture to bread pudding but full of fibre. Serve as a pudding with real custard if you want to be popular.

9.

YEASTED BUNS, FRUIT BREADS AND SCONES

The following recipes call for fresh yeast. If you wish to substitute dried yeast use half the amount given for fresh. Reconstitute by leaving to 'work', i.e. become active by soaking in a little warm water mixed with a sprinkle of sugar. Some recipes will only work with fresh yeast and this will be explained as it occurs. See notes on using the new 'instant' yeasts on page 15.

Remember dried active yeast that has been on the shop shelf too long will not be active whatever you do to coax it. This could lead to failures. Fresh yeast, if you can get it, should never fail you — it's what bakers use!

HOT CROSS BUNS

Imperial (Metric)
½ oz (15g) fresh yeast
Approx. ¼ pint (140ml) warm milk
¾ lb (340g) wholemeal flour
2 oz (55g) polyunsaturated
  margarine
2 oz (55g) raw cane sugar
1 egg, beaten
4 oz (115g) currants
½ level teaspoonful cinnamon
¾ level teaspoonful mixed spice
3 pinches grated nutmeg
Coarsely grated rind of 1 lemon and
  1 orange

American
1¼ tablespoonsful fresh yeast
Approx. ⅔ cupful warm milk
3 cupsful wholewheat flour
¼ cupful polyunsaturated margarine
⅓ cupful raw cane sugar
1 egg, beaten
⅔ cupful currants
½ level teaspoonful cinnamon
1 scant teaspoonful mixed spice
3 pinches grated nutmeg
Coarsely grated rind of 1 lemon and
  1 orange

1. Cream the yeast with some of the milk and a sprinkle of the sugar. Leave in a warm place to grow frothy.

2. Put the flour into a bowl and pour in the frothy yeast. Add the melted margarine, sugar, beaten egg, currants, spices and rinds. Mix/stir to a soft dough.

3. Knead on a floured worktop until the dough is smooth. Put back into the basin in the shape of a giant bun and leave in a warm place to rise, covered with a clean tea towel.

4. When doubled in size turn out on to a floured worktop again and this time knead only lightly.

5. Cut into 12 pieces and roll into balls. Place on greased baking trays, leaving enough space for them to increase in size. Flatten with your palm. Cut crosses with a knife and leave to rise in a warm place.

6. Bake in a preheated oven at 425°F/220°C (Gas Mark 7) above centre of oven for about 15 to 20 minutes.

7. Make a glaze of 1 tablespoonful each of milk, raw cane sugar and water, boiled in a small saucepan.

8. As soon as you take the buns out of the oven brush with the glaze to make them shiny.

9. Serve still warm from the oven and make them live up to their name. Some people like them just as they are, others prefer them split and buttered.

Note: Commercially-baked ones are usually very lacking in spices and fruit, so this recipe puts it all right. Traditional buns for Good Friday, just before Easter. Any left over can be eaten toasted the following day.

CURRANT BUNS

Britain imports over half the world's supply of currants, partly because currant buns are so popular. Make in the same way as Hot Cross Buns (page 126) but leave out the spices and rinds. (Also leave off the crosses.)

FRUIT BUNS

Make in the same way as Hot Cross Buns (page 126) but vary the fruit. Sultanas (golden seedless raisins), raisins, chopped dried apricots, pineapple and bananas. Omit the spices but include the rinds. Eat freshly baked or stale and toasted, split and buttered. Serve for tea or for a snack.

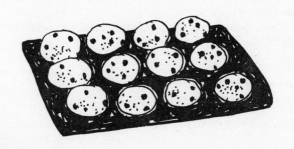

BATH BUNS

A West Country approach to the British bun. They can still be bought from bakeries in and around Bath, a famous English spa, and all over England. This wholefood version is a variation of the traditional Bath Bun. Note it does not contain any currants — one of its distinguishing features. Serve for tea, elevenses or as a snack, split and buttered. Eat freshly baked, or toasted the following day.

Imperial (Metric)	American
1 oz (30g) fresh yeast	2½ tablespoonsful fresh yeast
1 teaspoonful raw cane sugar	1 teaspoonful raw cane sugar
1 tablespoonful warm water	1 tablespoonful warm water
4 oz (115g) polyunsaturated margarine	⅔ cupful polyunsaturated margarine
8 fl oz (225ml) cold milk	1 cupful cold milk
2 eggs, beaten	2 eggs, beaten
1 lb (455g) wholemeal flour	4 cupsful wholewheat flour
4 oz (115g) raw cane sugar	⅔ cupful raw cane sugar
6 oz (170g) sultanas	1 cupful golden seedless raisins
Finely grated rind of 1 lemon	Finely grated rind of 1 lemon
1 tablespoonful milk, mixed with ½ beaten egg and raw cane sugar for top	1 tablespoonful milk mixed with ½ beaten egg and raw cane sugar for top

1. Cream the yeast with the teaspoonful of sugar and tablespoonful warm water. Leave to work until it froths.

2. Melt the margarine gently in a small saucepan and pour in the cold milk. Leave to cool and then add the beaten eggs. Whisk to combine.

3. Put the flour into a mixing bowl with the sugar, sultanas (golden seedless raisins) and lemon rind. Mix and make a well in the centre.

4. Pour in the egg mixture and then the frothy yeast. Mix well with a wooden spoon to a stiff dough.

5. Leave to rise in a warm place, covered with a clean tea towel.

6. When doubled in size, knead and shape into a long sausage. (You should not need too much flour as the dough should be elastic and shiny.) Cut into 12 pieces. Roll into balls and flatten with your palm to make into buns.

7. Place on greased baking trays, leaving enough space around each one for it to double in size.

8. Brush each bun with egg/milk glaze and sprinkle with the raw cane sugar.

9. Bake on the top shelf of a preheated oven at 375°F/190°C (Gas Mark 5) for about 15 to 20 minutes.

10. Take out of the oven and cool on a wire rack.

DUTCH DOUGHNUTS

This recipe is based on a traditional one from Holland where they are made and eaten on New Year's Eve.

Imperial (Metric)	American
1 oz (30g) fresh yeast*	2 tablespoonsful fresh yeast*
6 fl oz (170ml) scalded milk cooled down to lukewarm	¾ cupful scalded milk cooled down to lukewarm
1 large cooking apple	1 large cooking apple
Juice of 1 lemon	Juice of 1 lemon
Rind of ½ a lemon	Rind of ½ a lemon
Rind of ½ an orange	Rind of ½ an orange
1 egg, beaten	1 egg, beaten
2 oz (55g) raisins	⅓ cupful raisins
½ lb (225g) wholemeal flour	2 cupsful wholewheat flour
4 pinches cinnamon	4 pinches cinnamon
Fructose (optional)	Fructose (optional)

1. Cream the yeast with about a tablespoonful of the warm milk. Add a little more milk and leave to 'work' for a few minutes in a warm place.

2. Peel and core the apple. Grate coarsely and mix with the lemon juice, rinds and yeast mixture.

3. Add the beaten egg, raisins, flour and cinnamon plus the remaining milk and mix well.

4. Leave this dough to rise in a warm place, covered with a clean, damp tea towel.

5. Knead lightly and divide into pieces the size of a large walnut. (You will find this easiest if you first oil your hands lightly with cooking oil.)

6. Leave to rise for a few minutes in a warm place.

7. Drop them into deep, very hot oil. They will puff up as they cook. Remove quickly when golden and drain on kitchen paper.

8. Serve still warm, sprinkled with fructose (optional).

* Best made with fresh yeast, not the dried variety.

APRICOT AND WALNUT BREAD

A delicious combination of dried apricots and walnuts in a bread to serve buttered, for tea.

Imperial (Metric)	American
½ oz (15g) fresh yeast	1 tablespoonful fresh yeast
¼ pint (140ml) warm milk	⅔ cupful warm milk
½ lb (225g) wholemeal flour	2 cupsful wholewheat flour
2 heaped teaspoonsful raw cane sugar	2 heaped teaspoonsful raw cane sugar
4 oz (115g) chopped, dried apricots	⅔ cupful chopped, dried apricots
1 oz (30g) chopped walnuts	¼ cupful chopped English walnuts

1. Cream the yeast with a little of the warm milk and leave to get frothy.

2. Mix the flour and sugar in a bowl. Make a well in the centre.

3. Add the rest of the warm milk to the frothy yeast mixture and stir.

4. Pour into the flour and mix to a soft dough. Knead until smooth and put back into the bowl.

5. Leave in a warm place to rise, covered with a clean tea towel.

6. When the dough has risen and doubled in size, turn out on to a floured worktop.

7. Make slashes with a sharp knife and sprinkle in the fruit and nuts. Knead again until the dough is smooth and the fruit and nuts evenly distributed.

8. Shape into a fat sausage and put into a greased 1 lb (500g) loaf tin. Leave to rise in a warm place covered with a clean tea towel.

9. When the loaf has risen to the top of the tin, bake in a preheated oven at 425°F/220°C (Gas Mark 7), on the centre shelf, for about 45 minutes.

10. Turn out of the tin and cool on a wire rack.

11. Slice when cold and serve buttered.

DANISH PASTRIES

You will find these different from the commercially-made ones that feature all over Europe in bakers' shops. They make a delicious yeasted pastry to be eaten for tea or as a snack at elevenses or mid afternoon. Much less fat is used in this wholefood version and more filling. If the price of cardamom is too prohibitive, crush a couple of seeds (not pods) in a pestle and mortar.

Pastry:

Imperial (Metric)	American
½ lb (225g) wholemeal flour	2 cupsful wholewheat flour
3 level teaspoonsful raw cane sugar	3 level teaspoonsful raw cane sugar
5 pinches ground cardamom	5 pinches ground cardamom
½ oz (15g) fresh yeast	1¼ tablespoonsful fresh yeast
¼ pint (140ml) warm milk	⅔ cupful warm milk
2 oz (55g) polyunsaturated margarine, melted	5 tablespoonsful polyunsaturated margarine, melted
1 egg, beaten	1 egg, beaten

Filling:

Choose one from the list (page 133)

Topping:

A little raw cane sugar boiled in water for the glaze
Chopped nuts

1. Make the pastry. Put the flour, sugar and cardamom into a warm mixing bowl. Mix well.

2. Put the yeast into a basin and stir to a cream with a little of the milk. Leave to 'work'.

3. Pour in the melted margarine as soon as yeast has become frothy. Then add the beaten egg. Mix well.

4. Pour this over the flour mixture and mix to a paste. Knead to a smooth dough using more flour and leave to rise in a warm place, covered with a clean tea towel.

5. Make the filling.

6. When the dough has risen knead again and roll out to a rectangle about 10 × 15 in. (25 × 37cm). Do this on a well floured worktop.

7. Spread the dough with the filling and roll up like a Swiss-roll, using the longest side. Use a sharp knife to cut into slices.

8. Place on a greased baking sheet, leaving spaces between them as they will rise and expand. Leave to rise, uncovered in a warm place for about 15 minutes.

9. Bake on the top shelf of a preheated oven at 450°F/230°C (Gas Mark 8) for about 15 minutes.

10. Take out of the oven and put on to a wire rack to cool. You will probably find them easiest to remove from the baking sheet with a spatula.

11. Glaze with the sugar/water mix, using a pastry brush and sprinkle with the chopped nuts.

12. Eat freshly baked.

Fillings:

a) Home-made mincemeat.

b) Equal quantities of butter and raw cane sugar and currants. Cream the butter and sugar and spread over the pastry. Sprinkle with the currants and roll up. You can also add a little cinnamon to taste.

c) Soak dried fruits and cook in orange juice until they form a spreadable pulp. Sweeten with raw cane sugar and flavour with sugar to taste. Try apricots (favourite!) with sultanas (golden seedless raisins), chopped stoned prunes, or chopped pears/peaches with raisins. Stoned dates can be mixed with a little grated apple. The more exotic dried fruits can also be used such as pineapple.

Note: Whatever fruit or mixture of fruits you use aim for a final amount of about 4 tablespoonsful (heaped). If you find yourself short on the mixture add a little ground almond to make up the amount.

FRUIT PLAIT

This is adapted from a traditional recipe from Denmark. It will serve 8 to 10 for a very late breakfast, elevenses, snack or grand tea.

Pastry:

Imperial (Metric)	American
½ lb (225g) wholemeal flour	2 cupsful wholewheat flour
2 heaped teaspoonsful raw cane sugar	2 heaped teaspoonsful raw cane sugar
½ level teaspoonful cinnamon	½ level teaspoonful cinnamon
½ oz (15g) fresh yeast mixed to a cream with a little of the warm milk	2 tablespoonsful fresh yeast mixed to a cream with a little of the warm milk
2 oz (55g) polyunsaturated margarine, melted	5 tablespoonsful polyunsaturated margarine, melted
¼ pint (140ml) warm water or watered down milk	⅔ cupful warm water or watered down milk
1 egg, beaten	1 egg, beaten

Filling:

Imperial (Metric)	American
1 oz (30g) polyunsaturated margarine	2½ tablespoonsful polyunsaturated margarine
1 oz (30g) ground almonds	¼ cupful ground almonds
2 oz (55g) sultanas or chopped dried apricots	⅓ cupful golden seedless raisins or chopped dried apricots
1 eating apple, coarsely grated	1 eating apple, coarsely grated
½ level teaspoonful cinnamon	½ level teaspoonful cinnamon
2 oz (55g) raw cane sugar	⅓ cupful raw cane sugar
3 tablespoonsful orange juice	3 tablespoonsful orange juice

Topping:

Flaked (slivered) almonds and sugar glaze made by boiling a little raw cane sugar in water

1. To make pastry; put the flour, sugar, cinnamon into a warm mixing bowl and mix well.

2. When the yeast is frothy add to rest of the milk plus the margarine. Mix well.

3. Add the beaten egg to the milk mixture and mix again.

4. Pour over the flour mixture and stir/mix to a smooth paste.

5. Leave to rise in a warm place, covered with a clean tea-towel.

6. To make filling; cream the margarine and ground almonds in a small bowl.

7. Add all other ingredients and mix well.

8. When the pastry has risen, knead to a soft dough, using more flour.

9. Roll out into a rectangle 8×14 in. (20×35cm).

10. Put on to a greased sheet and spread the filling in a strip down the middle — 2 in. (5cm) wide.

11. With a sharp knife cut the pastry as shown and fold over filling to form a plait.

continued overleaf.

12. Brush with milk and sprinkle with flaked (slivered) almonds.

13. Put in a warm place, uncovered for about 15 minutes to rise.

14. Bake in a preheated oven 450°F/230°C (Gas Mark 8), top shelf, for about 15 minutes.

15. As soon as you take it out of the oven brush with the sugar glaze, adding a few more almonds if you wish.

16. Serve still warm from the oven with a knife and fork.

CHELSEA BUNS
Makes 18 small buns or 12 large

Imperial (Metric)	American
1 oz (30g) fresh yeast*	2½ tablespoonsful fresh yeast*
Warm milk	Warm milk
2 eggs, whisked	2 eggs, whisked
4 oz (115g) polyunsaturated margarine	½ cupful polyunsaturated margarine
1 lb (455g) wholemeal flour	4 cupsful wholewheat flour
2 oz (55g) raw cane sugar	⅓ cupful raw cane sugar
Grated rind of 1 lemon	Grated rind of 1 lemon
1 teaspoonful mixed spice	1 teaspoonful mixed spice

Filling:

Imperial (Metric)	American
3 oz (85g) each of:	⅓ cupful each of:
currants	currants
melted polyunsaturated margarine	melted polyunsaturated margarine
raw cane sugar	½ cupful raw cane sugar

Glaze:

Melted honey

1. Cream the yeast with a little of the warm milk and some of the sugar. Add a little more of the milk and leave to 'work' in a warm place.

2. Put the eggs, a little more warm milk and the melted margarine into a basin and mix well.

3. Put the flour into a mixing bowl and stir in the rest of the sugar, lemon rind and spice. Pour in the egg mixture and then the yeast. Add enough warm milk to make a firm dough. Mix and knead well.

4. Leave in a warm place, covered with a clean tea towel until just about doubled in size.

5. Knead the dough lightly and divide into 2 equal-sized pieces. Roll out into 2 rectangles, about 10×14 in. (25×35cm).

6. Brush with the melted margarine and sprinkle with the filling ingredients — currants and sugar.

7. Roll up like a Swiss-roll (starting with the short edge).

8. Cut into slices and place on greased baking trays so that when risen they will be touching. Allow for doubling in size (area and height).

9. Leave to rise in a warm place.

10. Bake in a preheated oven at 425°F/220°C (Gas Mark 7), on the top shelf, for about 15 to 20 minutes.

11. Brush with glaze and serve warm or at least on the day they are baked.

* If using 'instant' yeast you will only need half the amount given for fresh yeast. Ignore stage 1 and put in all the milk at stage 2. Add the instant yeast dry to the flour at stage 3 and then proceed as main recipe. Using 'instant' yeast will give you quicker rising.

Note: Correct positioning of the buns before the last rising will cause them to spread into squares that can be broken apart. This does not affect the taste one little bit but it does make them look like Chelsea buns!

BRIXTON BUNS

Use the Chelsea Buns recipe but instead of currants use chopped dried bananas and instead of the mixed spice use cinnamon. Chopped dried pineapple and papaya can also be used.

PLUM BREAD

Bursting with as much fruit as a cake and with old-fashioned tea time nostalgia, here is a tea bread that will keep its good nature for several days. As it contains baking powder as well as yeast it is not left to rise before baking. The yeast *must* be fresh and not the dried variety. The lined tin will ensure it turns out easily. This recipe is high in fibre.

Imperial (Metric)	American
¾ lb (340g) wholemeal flour	3 cupsful wholewheat flour
2 level teaspoonsful baking powder	2 level teaspoonsful baking powder
1 level teaspoonful mixed spice	1 level teaspoonful mixed spice
4 oz (115g) polyunsaturated margarine	½ cupful polyunsaturated margarine
4 oz (115g) sultanas	⅔ cupful golden seedless raisins
4 oz (115g) chopped, dried apricots	⅔ cupful chopped, dried apricots
6 oz (170g) currants	1 cupful currants
3 oz (85g) raisins	½ cupful raisins
2 oz (55g) chopped dates	⅓ cupful chopped dates
Grated rind of 1 orange	Grated rind of 1 orange
6 oz (170g) raw cane sugar	1 cupful raw cane sugar
½ pint (285ml) warm milk	1⅓ cupsful warm milk
1 oz (30g) fresh yeast	2½ tablespoonsful fresh yeast

1. Preheat oven at 300°F/150°C (Gas Mark 2).

2. Grease a 2 lb (1kg) loaf tin and line just the bottom with greased greaseproof paper.

3. Put the flour, baking powder and spice into a mixing bowl.

4. Add the margarine and rub in with the fingers.

5. Stir in all the fruit and rind. Add the sugar except for approx. 1 tablespoonful. Mix well.

6. Sprinkle the tablespoonful of sugar into the warm milk and stir until it has dissolved.

7. Finely crumble the yeast and sprinkle into the milk mixture. Stir well.

8. Pour this into the dry ingredients and mix with a wooden spoon to quite a stiff dough.

9. Turn into the prepared tin and bake slowly on the centre shelf of the oven for about 2 hours.

10. Leave to cool in the tin.

11. Serve as a teabread, sliced and buttered.

FRUIT LOAF

A semi-sweet bread enriched with dried fruit. Serve buttered, or when stale, toasted and buttered. A traditional British tea bread.

Imperial (Metric)	American
1 lb (455g) wholemeal flour	4 cupsful wholewheat flour
2 oz (55g) polyunsaturated margarine	¼ cupful polyunsaturated margarine
3 oz (85g) sultanas	½ cupful golden seedless raisins
3 oz (85g) currants	½ cupful currants
Grated rind of 1 orange or 1 lemon	Grated rind of 1 orange or 1 lemon
2 oz (55g) raw cane sugar	⅓ cupful raw cane sugar
½ oz (15g) fresh yeast*	1 tablespoonful fresh yeast*
2 eggs	2 eggs
4 fl oz (115ml) warm milk	½ cupful warm milk
Melted honey for glaze	Melted honey for glaze

1. Put the flour and margarine into a bowl. Rub in with the fingers.

2. Put all the fruit and rind into the mixture with all but a teaspoonful of the sugar. Mix well.

3. Cream the yeast with the teaspoonful of sugar.

4. Beat the eggs with the warm milk and stir in the creamed yeast. Leave for a few minutes for the yeast to 'work'.

5. Add to the rest of the ingredients in the bowl and mix to a soft dough. Knead well on a floured worktop.

6. Put back into the bowl and cover with a clean cloth. Leave to rise in a warm place, until doubled in size.

7. Knead again and put into a greased loaf tin. Leave to rise for about 15 minutes, in a warm place.

8. Bake in a preheated oven 425°F/220°C (Gas Mark 7) for the first 10 or 12 minutes. Then lower the heat to 400°F/200°C (Gas Mark 6) for another 40 to 45 minutes.

9. When the loaf is nearly done take out of the oven and glaze the top with melted honey. Put back in the oven for another 5 minutes.

10. When baked, turn out of the tin and cool on a wire rack.

* If 'instant' yeast is available use half the amount given for fresh yeast and sprinkle it in at stage 2 with all the sugar. Omit stage 3. For stage 4 just beat the eggs and milk and add immediately to the rest of the ingredients. Proceed to stage 5, etc. 'Instant' yeast will enable you to make this loaf much more quickly.

ORANGE AND RAISIN PLAIT

Imperial (Metric)	American
1 lb (455g) wholemeal flour	4 cupsful wholewheat flour
2 tablespoonsful raw cane sugar	2 tablespoonsful raw cane sugar
2 oz (55g) raisins	1/3 cupful raisins
1 oz (30g) fresh yeast	2 1/2 tablespoonsful fresh yeast
1 teaspoonful raw cane sugar	1 teaspoonful raw cane sugar
Juice and finely grated rind of 2 oranges (small)	Juice and finely grated rind of 2 oranges (small)
1/2 cupful warm water, or more	1/2 cupful warm water, or more
1 egg, beaten	1 egg, beaten

Glaze:
1 tablespoonful milk
1 level tablespoonful raw cane sugar
1 tablespoonful water

1. Put the flour, sugar and raisins into a bowl. Mix well and make a well in the centre.

2. Put the yeast into a small basin with the teaspoonful of sugar and stir to a cream.

3. Add a little of the warm water and leave to get frothy.

4. When ready, stir in the orange juice, rind and beaten egg.

5. Pour this mixture into the flour and make into a soft dough with the rest of the warm water.

6. Knead on a floured worktop until the dough feels smooth.

7. Put back into the bowl and cover with a clean tea towel. Leave in a warm place to rise.

8. When the dough has risen to double its size, knead again and divide into 3 equally-sized pieces.

9. Roll each piece into a long sausage and place on a greased baking sheet.

10. Seal three ends together by pinching them and then plait into a loaf. Make the shape of the plait widest in the middle to give the loaf a long oval shape.

11. Seal the ends and leave in a warm place, uncovered, to rise.

12. Bake in a preheated oven at 425°F/220°C (Gas Mark 7), above centre of the oven, for about 30 minutes.

13. Boil the glaze ingredients in a small saucepan for a couple of minutes.

14. Brush the plait with the glaze as soon as you take it out of the oven and put it on a wire rack to cool.

15. When cold, break into pieces or slices and serve with butter.

Variation: Try Lemon and Apricot Plait. Use 1 lemon instead of 2 oranges but increase the amount of sugar to 3 tablespoonsful. For the fruit use chopped, dried apricots.

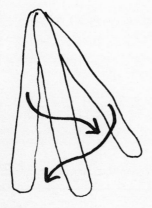

FRUIT BANNOCK

From Scotland, a wholesome fruit bread in the shape of a large bun that will cut into long, oval slices. Choose a good quality flour that will give you the best flavour.

Imperial (Metric)	American
½ lb (225g) wholemeal flour	2 cupsful wholewheat flour
1½ oz (45g) polyunsaturated margarine	4 tablespoonsful polyunsaturated margarine
¼ pint (140ml) warm milk	⅔ cupful warm milk
1½ oz (45g) raw cane sugar	¼ cupful raw cane sugar
½ oz (15g) fresh yeast	1¼ tablespoonsful fresh yeast
4 oz (115g) sultanas	⅔ cupful golden seedless raisins
Warm runny honey or beaten egg for glaze	Warm runny honey or beaten egg for the glaze

1. Put the flour into a mixing bowl and rub in the margarine.

2. Pour the warm milk into a basin and stir in the sugar until dissolved. Sprinkle in the yeast (after crumbling) and leave to 'work' in a warm place for a few minutes.

3. When frothy, pour into the flour mixture. Mix well until the dough is smooth.

4. Use a little more flour to knead into 1 ball and leave in a warm place, covered with a clean tea towel.

5. Cut the dough with a knife and sprinkle in the fruit, pressing it into the cuts. Knead back into shape and leave to rise again.

6. Knead for the last time and shape into a ball. Any fruit that detaches itself from the dough can be pressed back in. Grease a baking sheet and place the bannock on this, leaving it to rise after flattening.

7. Brush gently with the glaze of your choice and bake in a preheated oven at 425°F/220°C (Gas Mark 7) for 20 to 25 minutes, centre shelf.

8. Leave to cool on a wire rack. Eat freshly baked, sliced and buttered. Use for tea or for a snack. Stale bannock can be toasted.

If using 'instant' yeast you will need ½ tablespoonful.

1. Mix the flour, yeast and sugar in a bowl.

2. Rub in the margarine and add the milk. Mix to a smooth dough and proceed as for the main recipe, as from stage 4. With this type of yeast the bannock will not take quite so long to make.

IRISH FRUIT LOAF

The inclusion of mashed potato in this recipe is the clue to its Irish origin. It is still eaten for tea sitting round the open peat fire with the kettle singing on the hob ready to make the tea. After a day in the rain cutting peat or gathering seaweed it tastes wonderful! Even if there is no fruit to put in this bread the Irish still call it 'fruit loaf'. However, the fruit version is by far the best.

Imperial (Metric)	American
1 oz (30g) fresh yeast*	2 tablespoonsful fresh yeast*
3 tablespoonsful potato water	3 tablespoonsful potato water
1 heaped tablespoonful warm, mashed potato	1 heaped tablespoonful warm, mashed potato
3 tablespoonsful honey	3 tablespoonsful honey
10 oz (285g) wholemeal flour	2½ cupsful wholewheat flour
2 oz (55g) polyunsaturated margarine	¼ cupful polyunsaturated margarine
1 egg, beaten	1 egg, beaten
3 oz (85g) raisins	½ cupful raisins

1. Put the yeast into a bowl with the potato water and stir until creamy.

2. Add the mashed potatoes, half the honey and just under half the flour. Mix until smooth.

3. Leave to rise in a warm place, covered with a clean tea towel.

4. Stir and beat in a little more of the flour.

5. Melt the margarine, gently, and let it cool. Add to the dough and mix well.

6. Stir in the beaten egg and the rest of the honey.

7. Lastly put in the raisins and the final portion of the flour. Mix to a soft dough, then knead on a floured worktop for a few minutes.

8. Oil a bowl and put in the dough. Turn it over once so that it has all come in contact with the oil.

9. Cover and leave again in a warm place to rise. This should take about an hour.

10. Pull the dough into 1 piece, i.e. knock it down and put into a greased 2 lb (1 kg) loaf tin to rise for the last time.

11. Cover with a clean tea towel and leave to double in size.

12. Bake in a preheated oven 350°F/180°C (Gas Mark 4) for about an hour.

13. Serve sliced thickly and spread with butter.

*If using 'instant' yeast ignore stages 1 and 2. Use half the amount given for fresh yeast and mix it in dry with just under half the flour. Add the potato water, mashed potatoes and half the honey. Mix until smooth and proceed as from stage 3.

IRISH TEA BRACK

The whiskey in this recipe is often just a dream and all tea is used instead.

Imperial (Metric)
6 oz (170g) sultanas
6 oz (170g) raisins
4 oz (115g) honey
3 tablespoonsful whiskey + enough cold tea to make 1 pint (570ml)*
6 oz (170g) wholemeal flour
1 large or 2 small egg(s), beaten
1 level teaspoonful baking powder
Honey for glaze

American
1 cupful golden seedless raisins
1 cupful raisins
4 tablespoonsful honey
3 tablespoonsful whiskey + enough cold tea to make 2½ cupsful*
1½ cupsful wholewheat flour
1 large or 2 small egg(s), beaten
1 slightly heaped teaspoonful baking powder
Honey for glaze

1. Put the dried fruit into a bowl with the honey and liquids. Leave overnight to plump the fruit.

2. Preheat the oven at 300°F/150°C (Gas Mark 2).

3. Add alternate amounts of the flour and beaten egg to the bowl of fruit.

4. Last of all put in the baking powder and mix well.

5. Turn into a well greased 2 lb (1kg) loaf tin and bake for about 1½ hours, above centre of oven.

6. When baked, glaze with honey.

7. Serve sliced thickly and spread with butter — Irish if you can get it, for an authentic taste.

* Just plain tea, out of the teapot, without milk.

MALT BREAD

Imperial (Metric)	American
½ oz (30g) fresh yeast*	1 tablespoonful fresh yeast*
Warm water	Warm water
1 teaspoonful raw cane sugar	1 teaspoonful raw cane sugar
½ lb (225g) wholemeal flour	2 cupsful wholewheat flour
1 teaspoonful mixed spice	1 teaspoonful mixed spice
4 oz (115g) seedless raisins	⅔ cupful seedless raisins
1 oz (30g) butter	2½ tablespoonsful butter
1 tablespoonful black treacle	1 tablespoonful molasses
1 large tablespoonful malt extract	1 large tablespoonful malt extract
Warm milk	Warm milk
Honey for glaze	Honey for glaze

1. Cream the yeast in a cup with the sugar. Add a little warm water and leave to work for a few minutes, until frothy.

2. Mix the flour and spice in a bowl.

3. Sprinkle in the raisins.

4. Put the butter, black treacle (molasses) and malt into a small saucepan. Heat gently, mix well and leave to cool.

5. Spoon into the flour mixture. Add the yeast liquid and mix to a soft dough with warm milk.

6. Leave to rise in a warm place, covered with a cloth.

7. Knead. Grease a small loaf tin and put the dough into this. Leave to rise again.

8. Bake in a preheated oven 400°F/200°C (Gas Mark 6) for about 40 to 45 minutes.

9. Turn out of the tin and cool on a wire rack. Cut when cold.

10. Slice thickly and serve spread with butter or margarine.

* If using 'instant' yeast you will need only ½ tablespoonful. Ignore stage 1. Add the yeast at stage 2 and omit sugar from the recipe.

MUESLI BREAD
Makes 1 loaf

It would be difficult to find a nuttier bread and the added raisins give interest to an otherwise brown loaf. Serve it for Sunday breakfast and save lots of washing up!

Imperial (Metric)	American
¼ oz (7g) fresh yeast*	½ tablespoonful fresh yeast*
2 heaped tablespoonsful raw cane sugar	2 heaped tablespoonsful raw cane sugar
½ pint (285ml) warm milk	1⅓ cupsful warm milk
10 oz (285g) wholemeal flour	2½ cupsful wholewheat flour
1 tablespoonful wheat bran	1 tablespoonful wheat bran
1 heaped tablespoonful raisins	1 heaped tablespoonful raisins
2 tablespoonsful muesli (see page 158)	2 tablespoonsful muesli (see page 158)
½ an eating apple	½ an eating apple
Honey for glaze (optional)	Honey for glaze (optional)

1. Crumble the yeast into a cup with the sugar and pour on 3 or 4 tablespoonsful of the warm milk. Mix and leave to froth.

2. Put the flour and bran into a warm mixing bowl and grate in the apple.

3. When the yeast has 'worked' pour into a well in the centre of the flour mixture.

4. Combine, adding the rest of the warm milk to make a soft dough. Knead well and leave in a warm place, covered with a clean tea towel. Let the dough double in size.

5. Work in the raisins and muesli, after chopping any large nuts, and knead again.

6. Shape into a fat sausage and put into a greased 1 lb (500g) loaf tin. Cover and leave to rise in a warm place.

7. Bake in a preheated oven 425°F/220°C (Gas Mark 7) for about 40 minutes.

8. Turn out of the tin and leave to cool on a wire rack, glazing with the melted honey if you wish.

9. Serve sliced and buttered and spread with honey on the day of baking and toasted and buttered the following day.

* If using 'instant' yeast the method is slightly different. Use just one slightly heaped teaspoonful of instant yeast.

1. Put the yeast, sugar, flour, bran and grated apple into a bowl and mix well.

2. Pour in the warm milk and mix to a soft dough. Leave to rise in a warm place and then proceed as from stage 5 in the main recipe.

BARA BRITH

Makes 1 small loaf

Traditional 'Speckled Bread' from Wales.

Imperial (Metric)	American
1½ oz (45g) butter	3½ tablespoonsful butter
¼ pint (140ml) warm milk (or more)	⅔ cupful warm milk (or more)
4 pinches grated nutmeg	4 pinches grated nutmeg
½ lb (225g) wholemeal flour	2 cupsful wholewheat flour
¼ oz (7g) fresh yeast	½ tablespoonful fresh yeast
Any mixture dried fruit to make 3 oz (75g)	Any mixture dried fruit to make ½ cupful
1 small egg, beaten	1 small egg, beaten
1 tablespoonful runny honey	1 generous tablespoonful runny honey

1. Put the butter into a small saucepan and melt gently.

2. Add the milk and stir well. Cool (if necessary) to lukewarm.

3. Put the nutmeg and flour into a bowl and mix. Crumble the yeast finely and then sprinkle it in. Stir in the dried fruit.

4. Beat the egg in a basin and add the warm milk/butter mixture, with the honey. Mix well. (If it is too stiff add more warm milk.)

5. Pour on to the flour mixture and stir. Leave to rise in a warm place, covered with a clean tea towel.

6. When the dough has risen to double the size, knead on a floured worktop. Shape into a fat sausage and put into a greased 1 lb (500g) loaf tin. Leave to rise again.

7. Preheat oven at 350°F/180°C (Gas Mark 4).

8. Bake above centre of oven for about 30 minutes.

9. Turn out of the tin as soon as you take it out of the oven. Serve for tea, buttered. Stale Bara Brith can be toasted and buttered.

Note: This is a very simple traditional loaf that allows the cook to be flexible in the choice of fruits — e.g. what ever happens to be in the cupboard. An up-to-date version could include some of the more exotic fruits. (This recipe calls for fresh bakers' yeast, not dried.)

WELSH CAKES

For this recipe you will need a griddle to cook the scones. If you don't own one of these a heavy based frying pan (skillet) can be used instead. Cook the scones (cakes) on the hottest part of the griddle at first to crisp the outsides. Then, move to the part which is less hot so that the centres can cook through. Each scone will take 5 minutes on each side over a medium heat.

Imperial (Metric)	American
½ lb (225g) wholemeal flour	2 cupsful wholewheat flour
2 teaspoonsful baking powder	2 slightly heaped teaspoonsful baking powder
1 oz (30g) butter	2½ tablespoonsful butter
2 oz (55g) currants	⅓ cupful currants
1 tablespoonful raw cane sugar	1 tablespoonful raw cane sugar
1 egg	1 egg
Approx. ¼ pint (140ml) cold milk	Approx. ⅔ cupful cold milk

1. Put the flour into a bowl with the baking powder. Mix well.

2. Add the butter and rub in with the fingers until the mixture resembles fine breadcrumbs.

3. Mix in the fruit and sugar.

4. Beat the egg and add to the mixture with enough of the milk to make a soft dough.

5. Knead and roll out, using more flour, to about ¼ in. (6mm) thick.

6. Cut into rounds and bake on an oiled griddle, turning once.

7. Serve hot or cold, spread with butter or polyunsaturated margarine.

Variation: Ideal for a snack or for tea. Sultanas (golden seedless raisins) can be used instead of currants, or small seedless raisins.

SINGIN' HINNY

This is a type of scone from the North of England that is baked on
the top of the stove and not in the oven. It's curious name comes
from the singing noise it makes during baking. Makes a good substitute
for bread if you have run out and several people turn up for tea. Very
filling.

Imperial (Metric)	American
7 oz (200g) wholemeal flour	1¾ cupsful wholewheat flour
2 teaspoonsful baking powder	2 teaspoonsful baking powder
½ teaspoonful sea salt	½ teaspoonful sea salt
2 oz (55g) polyunsaturated margarine	5 tablespoonsful polyunsaturated margarine
2 oz (55g) raw cane sugar	⅓ cupful raw cane sugar
3 oz (85g) currants	½ cupful currants
½ pint (¼ litre) milk	1⅓ cupsful milk

1. Put the flour and baking powder into a bowl with the salt. Mix.

2. Rub in the margarine.

3. Stir in the sugar and currants.

4. Make a well in the centre and pour in most of the milk.

5. Mix to a soft dough, adding as much milk as you need.

6. Form into 1 ball of dough and knead on a floured worktop.

7. Roll out to ¼ in. (6mm) thick, in a round.

8. Cut into wedges and cook on a heated griddle which has been
   well greased. (If you don't have a griddle a heavy-based frying
   pan or skillet will do.) After 4 or 5 minutes, turn with a spatula.

9. Cook on the other side for another 4 or 5 minutes when they
   should be risen and brown.

10. Serve right away, split and buttered.

Variation: Add 3 good pinches of mixed spice or cinnamon to the
flour. Sultanas (golden seedless raisins) can be used instead of currants
or a mixture of both. A sociable kind of scone that lends itself to tea
in the kitchen so everyone can hear the scones singing.

FRUIT SCONES

For the fruit in this recipe use currants, sultanas (golden seedless raisins) chopped dried apricots, raisins or chopped (stoned) prunes. Any mixture will do providing it weighs 2 oz (55g).

Imperial (Metric)	American
½ lb (225g) wholemeal flour	2 cupsful wholewheat flour
1 level teaspoonful baking powder	2 level teaspoonsful baking powder
3 pinches sea salt	3 pinches sea salt
2 oz (55g) polyunsaturated margarine	5 tablespoonsful polyunsaturated margarine
1 oz (30g) raw cane sugar	2½ tablespoonsful raw cane sugar
2 oz (55g) dried fruit	⅓ cupful dried fruit
1 egg, beaten	1 egg, beaten
Approx. ¼ pint (140ml) milk	Approx. ⅔ cupful milk
Honey for glaze	Honey for glaze

1. Preheat oven at 425°F/220°C (Gas Mark 7).

2. Put baking sheet in the oven to heat.

3. Mix flour, baking powder and salt in a mixing bowl.

4. Rub in margarine until mixture resembles fine breadcrumbs.

5. Stir in the sugar and fruit.

6. Mix to a soft dough with the beaten egg and as much milk as you need.

7. Knead quickly on a floured worktop.

8. Roll out and cut into rounds with a cutter, or, shape into 1 large round ½ in. (1cm) thick and cut into wedges with a sharp knife dipped in flour.

9. Place on the heated baking sheet and brush with melted honey.

10. Bake on the top shelf for about 15 to 20 minutes.

11. Serve split and buttered, freshly baked.

Note: Serve at tea-time or for a snack. Best still warm from the oven.

FRUIT MUFFINS
Makes 6

Serve for tea on frosty winter days. Leave out the spice and serve for breakfast, freshly baked, allowing two per person. The flour and fruits in this recipe make it a high-fibre one.

Imperial (Metric)	American
4 oz (115g) wholemeal flour	1 cupful wholewheat flour
2 teaspoonsful baking powder	2½ teaspoonsful baking powder
3 good pinches mixed spice or cinnamon	3 good pinches mixed spice or cinnamon
1½ oz (45g) polyunsaturated margarine	3 tablespoonsful polyunsaturated margarine
2 oz (55g) sultanas	⅓ cupful golden seedless raisins
1 heaped tablespoonful raw cane sugar	1 heaped tablespoonful raw cane sugar
1 small cooking apple, finely grated	1 small cooking apple, finely grated
1 egg	1 egg

1. Preheat oven at 450°F/230°C (Gas Mark 8).

2. Put the flour, baking powder and spice into a bowl. Mix.

3. Rub in the margarine, then stir in the dried fruit and sugar.

4. Beat the egg and use to mix all ingredients, including the grated apple, to a soft dough.

5. Knead into 1 ball of dough and then place on a floured worktop.

6. Either roll out or flatten by hand to a thickness of ½ in. (1cm). Cut into rounds and place on a greased baking sheet.

7. Bake the muffins above centre of the oven for about 15 minutes.

8. Serve still warm from the oven, split and buttered.

Note: If the dough turns out too soft at stage 4 then add a little more of the flour. Cooks in a hurry will prefer to break the dough into 6 pieces and shape into muffins individually. These are not so neat but save time.

10.

SNACKS AND DRINKS

Mueslis

What a godsend to the breakfast cereal manufacturers muesli has been. A chance to use up all the odds and ends of manufacture with an attractive label and wholesome title! But how much nicer (and with identifiable ingredients) is home-made muesli. As it needs no cooking, and very little preparation, it is an ideal breakfast for those in a hurry. Nutritionally it can be excellent too with a good balance of protein, carbohydrate, and a generous amount of fibre. Fresh and dried fruit add the minerals and vitamins needed (particularly iron in the dried fruit) and provided you don't smother it in cream, or add too many nuts it will be low in fat too. Salt is left out entirely, unlike commercially-made mueslis which can have a high salt content. You can also, of course, control the amount of sugar that goes into it. With all these virtues in mind it is as well to know about the basic design of a muesli.

First you should have a dry cereal base with at least one kind of dried fruit. To this is added one or two kinds of fresh fruit. Sugar or honey is used to sweeten them slightly and either milk or fruit juice is poured over to moisten them — just like you would over an ordinary breakfast cereal. In the very simplest type of muesli oats, nuts and a dried fruit are used, but for a more luxurious kind the dried fruit can be increased to 3 or 4 varieties and seeds as well as nuts can be added to the dry ingredients. The most popular fresh fruits to use with muesli are apple and banana but all kinds of fresh fruits in season can be used — pears, melon, strawberries, peaches, raspberries, etc.

Although muesli can give us such a good start to the day, like anything else, the same old thing, day in day out, can get boring. The secret is variety both in the bases and additions. A variety of bases (dry ingredients) can be made up and stored in airtight jars. These can be used as required. Just put 1 or 2 tablespoonsful into a cereal bowl, add the fresh fruit of your choice, either whole, chopped or sliced, as appropriate. Sweeten to taste and pour over milk or fruit juice. Some people prefer to moisten the dry ingredients and leave them overnight, covered, in the fridge, adding the fresh fruit next morning — resulting in a kind of fruity porridge.

MUESLI BASE I
Muesli in its most simple form.

4 heaped tablespoonsful rolled oats
2 heaped tablespoonsful chopped nuts
1 heaped tablespoonful raisins

1. Mix all together in an airtight container and use as required.

2. Use 1 or 2 tablespoonsful of the base and combine with chopped fresh apple, a little raw cane sugar or honey and milk to moisten.

MUESLI BASE II

4 heaped tablespoonsful rolled oats
2 heaped tablespoonsful chopped nuts
2 heaped tablespoonsful raisins
1 tablespoonful sultanas (golden seedless raisins)
8 dried apricots, chopped

1. Mix all ingredients in a bowl and transfer to a storage jar. Use as required with fresh fruit, honey and milk.

LUXURY MUESLI BASE

1 heaped tablespoonful wheat bran
3 heaped tablespoonsful rolled oats
1 heaped tablespoonful chopped hazelnuts
1 heaped tablespoonful cashews
1 heaped tablespoonful ground almonds
1 heaped tablespoonful raisins
1 heaped tablespoonful chopped dried apricots
1 heaped tablespoonful sunflower seeds
1 heaped tablespoonful sesame seeds

1. Mix all ingredients and keep in a storage jar. Use as required.

2. Put 1 to 2 tablespoonsful into a cereal bowl. Add raw cane sugar or honey, chopped fresh fruit and milk or fruit juice to moisten.

Sandwiches with Dried Fruit
Sandwiches consist of a filling arranged between two slices of buttered (or margarined) bread. Cut off the crusts if you prefer and make the fillings generous.

Fillings:
Cottage cheese and chopped dates.
Cheddar cheese and sultanas (golden seedless raisins).
Mashed hard-boiled egg and a chopped dried apricot.
Cottage cheese, walnuts (English walnuts), chopped, and raisins.
Cheddar cheese, spring onion (scallions) and dried pineapple.
Egg slices, cress or watercress and chopped stoned prunes.
Lettuce, curd cheese and chopped dried peach.
Cheddar cheese and home-made chutney with dried fruit.
Mashed, hard-boiled egg, chopped watercress and home-made chutney with dried fruit.

TOASTED SANDWICHES

For this type of sandwich use a special toaster or grill the sandwich on both sides in a flameproof dish, under the grill. Use any of the suggested sandwich fillings but serve any lettuce, cress etc., as a garnish and not inside the sandwich.

CHEESE AND DATE SANDWICH

Spread 2 slices of wholemeal bread with polyunsaturated margarine. Between the unspread sides put a layer of grated Cheddar cheese with a stoned date, chopped small. Grill on both sides to make a crisp outer and melted filling. Serve hot, right away.

OPEN SANDWICHES

These are made on a base of bread, spread with polyunsaturated margarine. This keeps the bread from going soggy. On top of this what would normally be the filling is arranged attractively in layers. The value of dried fruit in this context is really a garnish.

OPEN SALAD SANDWICHES

1. 1 slice wholemeal bread, spread lightly with polyunsaturated margarine, topped with a lettuce leaf (or leaves) to cover the whole slice, sliced tomatoes, a spoonful cottage cheese and a garnish of raisins and cucumber slices.

2. 1 slice wholemeal bread, spread lightly with polyunsaturated margarine, topped with watercress sprigs, slices of hard-boiled egg and garnished with tomato and sultanas (golden seedless raisins).

3. Instead of using salad greens as a base, mash a hard-boiled egg and mix with a little plain yogurt. Sprinkle with a few pinches of mild curry powder and mix well. Spread on the bread base. Top with sliced tomato, sultanas (golden seedless raisins), chopped onion and watercress sprigs.

HOT SAVOURY SPREADS

This is the open sandwich idea with a topping that goes under the grill. They are easiest to make in a food processor which will chop everything up in no time but they can be made by hand too. Make the spread and then pile thickly on to wholemeal toast and put under the grill until cooked. Serve with a green salad for an interesting snack lunch.

Spreads:

Mix the following and chop well.

1. Grated Cheddar cheese, tomato celery, mushroom, cucumber and watercress, sprinkle of raisins.

2. Cottage cheese, stoned dates (1 per portion), onion (small slice), tomato, celery, sprig of parsley, pineapple.

3. Tomato, small slice of onion and a sprig of parsley. Mix and then top with grated Cheddar cheese, mixed with chopped stoned prune as a garnish.

FRUIT SPREADS

Not all sandwiches are savoury. Try a sweeter version with one of these spreads, on its own or combined with cottage cheese.

Soak the fruit overnight in water. The next day drain and add fruit juice. Cook in a saucepan until soft. Mash with a fork and use, when cold, as a spread. Try these combinations:

Dried apricots and orange juice.

Raisins, orange juice and grated orange rind.

Stoned prunes and lemon juice with grated lemon rind.

Stoned dates and either orange or pineapple juice.

COCKTAIL NIBBLES

As a party treat, use a grapefruit to display cocktail sticks threaded with cubes of Cheddar cheese and pieces of dried apricot, stoned small prunes with fresh pineapple. Soak the fruit in hot water for an hour. Drain, pat dry with kitchen paper and use.

STUFFED PRUNES

Soak stoned prunes for about 6 hours in water so that they swell up. Drain and dry on kitchen paper. Open and fill the cavities left by the stones with cream cheese, marzipan, or walnut (English walnut) halves.

STUFFED DATES

Use large, good quality dates. Remove the stones and stuff the cavities with almond paste or almonds.

DRIED FRUIT YOGURT

Using dried fruit to flavour yogurt is an idea largely ignored by commercial yogurt companies. Some interesting combinations can be made which will add variety for yogurt fans and those who don't like the commercial fruit yogurts, which are all too often like flavoured toothpaste.

As a base use either home-made plain yogurt or commercial unflavoured yogurt. Here are some flavours to try:

Chopped fresh eating apple and a chopped, stoned date.

Chopped prune and walnut (English walnut).

Chopped dried apricot with a squeeze of fresh lemon juice.

Chopped, cooked fig and orange rind, finely grated.

Chopped, cooked dried peaches.

Chopped, cooked dried pear with a pinch of cinnamon.

Chopped, dried fruit salad.

Spoonful of home-made muesli and chopped apple.

Chopped eating apple and raisins or sultanas (golden seedless raisins) with a pinch of cinnamon.

Chopped fresh melon and chopped date.

FRUIT AND NUTS SNACKS

Eat a small amount of any of the following mixtures with a fresh eating apple or pear as a nutritious snack.

Dried apricots (small halves), hazelnuts, almonds and raisins.
Sultanas (golden seedless raisins), cashews and chopped Brazils with chopped dried prunes.
Hazelnuts and raisins.
Dried apricots and almonds.
Walnuts (English walnuts), sunflower seeds, raisins and sultanas (golden seedless raisins).

DRIED FRUIT SWEETS

Imperial (Metric)	American
½ lb (225g) dried fruit	1½ cupsful dried fruit
Honey	Honey
Desiccated coconut	Desiccated coconut

1. Soak the larger fruits such as apricots, prunes, etc. in cold water for about an hour to soften them.

2. Put all fruit through a mincer up to three times and mix well to blend, using a little honey if needed.

3. Form into balls and roll in the coconut.

4. Serve in small paper cases.

Note: The dried fruit can be any mixture of apricots, stoned prunes, figs, pears, raisins, etc.

YOGURT FRUIT DRINKS

Cook dried fruit such as apricots, stoned prunes, peaches and nectarines. Cool and put into a blender with raw cane sugar to taste, enough water to cover and a little unflavoured low-fat yogurt. Blend and thin down with skimmed milk to make a refreshing snack/drink.

FRUIT COOLER

Fill a whisky tumbler two-thirds full with crushed ice. Add dried apricot fruit juice* to come three-quarters up the glass and add a dash of apricot brandy.

Vary the fruit and use ordinary brandy. Try prune, nectarine and pear.

* Make the fruit juice by stewing soaked, dried fruit in water for 20 minutes. Allow to cool before liquidizing.

FRUIT MILK
Serves 2

Imperial (Metric)	American
½ pint (200ml) soaked, stewed and liquidized fruit	1⅓ cupsful soaked, stewed and liquidized fruit
½ pint (200ml) skimmed milk	1⅓ cupsful skimmed milk
Raw cane sugar to taste	Raw cane sugar to taste

1.   Blend in a liquidizer and serve in tall glasses.

Note: Best fruits to use are apricot, prune (with a little lemon juice and no sugar), peach, pear and nectarine. If the dried fruit juice doesn't make up to the required amount add a little fresh juice such as orange or a few slices of fresh banana.

PEACH AMBROSIA
Serves 4

Imperial (Metric)	American
1 pint (570ml) peach juice*	2½ cupsful peach juice*
¾ pint (425ml) skimmed milk	2 cupsful skimmed milk
2 or 3 teaspoonsful runny honey	2 or 3 teaspoonsful runny honey
1 tablespoonful single cream	1 tablespoonful light cream
2 egg whites	2 egg whites
Pinch of nutmeg	Pinch of nutmeg

1. Blend to a froth and serve in tall glasses.

Variation: The nutmeg can be added as a light dusting on top of the froth instead of being blended with the rest of the ingredients.

* Peach juice can be made from 6 to 8 dried peach halves soaked overnight, stewed in water, cooled and liquidized.

JAMAICA MILK SHAKE
Serves 2

Blend 1 banana, about 12 raisins, ¾ pint/425ml (2 cupsful) milk and a teaspoonful of lemon juice. (The raisins can be soaked overnight.)

DRIED FRUIT JUICES
It is sad to see so little use of dried fruits in juices. This is probably because most people feel the value of fruit juice to be in the vitamin C content. This is either very low or non-existent in dried fruits. However, it is worth remembering dried fruits can be a valuable source of other vitamins and minerals and their vitamin C content can always be supplemented by adding another kind of fresh juice. They combine well with other fresh fruits too — orange, apple, pear, peach, nectarine, strawberries, raspberries, blackberries, etc.

Dried fruit juice is easy to make as it only requires soaking overnight and then liquidizing next day. Make the juice in this way. Wash the dried fruit of your choice and then put into a basin with water to more than cover the fruit. Soak for at least 12 hours to soften the fruit. Blend/liquidize with the soaking water. (Large pieces of fruit should be chopped before soaking as this will help with the liquidizing and avoid lumps.) Add a little honey or raw cane sugar if you need to sweeten the juice. Either thin down with water or use another kind of fruit juice if you need to dilute it. If using dried fruit and fresh fruit to make a blend put the soaked dried fruit into the blender with the fresh fruit, cut into pieces. Add water or fruit juice to cover and blend all in one go. Sweeten with honey or raw cane sugar to taste.

Here is a reminder of the nutritional value of dried fruit juices. Sultanas and raisins contain copper, iron, calcium, magnesium, phosphorus, sodium, potassium, vitamins A, B_1, B_2, B_3 and B_6. The seedless varieties of raisin and all varieties of sultanas also contain vitamin B_6. Dried apricots, peaches, pears and nectarines contain calcium, iron, magnesium, phosphorus, sodium, potassium, vitamin A, B_1, B_2, B_3. Prunes are high in potassium and vitamin A and are a good source of iron.

Here are a few suggestions for blends you may like to try:

Raisin Juice: If you want a good iron content choose the seedless variety. Drink on its own or combine with fresh orange juice, 2 parts orange juice to 1 part raisin juice. Also very good with apple juice, 3 parts apple juice to 1 part raisin juice.

Prune Juice: This has an extremely strong taste so can be well diluted with water and a dash of fresh lemon juice. Combines well with grapefruit or orange juice. Use 3 parts fresh fruit juice to 1 part prune juice.

Dried Apricot Juice: Drink diluted with water and a dash of lemon juice. You may need to sweeten with a little runny honey. Combine it with fresh strawberry, raspberry, orange, peach or nectarine juice.

Sultana Juice: This will combine well with orange or pineapple juice. Use 2 parts sultanas (golden seedless raisins) juice to 2 parts fresh fruit juice and dilute with water if necessary. Excellent with apple juice (1 part sultana juice to 3 parts apple juice). A pinch of cinnamon can be added too.

Dried Peach Juice: This is delicious on its own or combined with strawberries or raspberries. Use 3 parts peach juice to 1 part fresh fruit juice. Try it with blackberry juice in the autumn, using a few fresh blackberries. Strain if you don't want the little pips.

Dried Pear Juice: This is delicious on its own with just a pinch of cinnamon to bring out the flavour. It combines best with small amounts of other dried fruit juices, for example, raisin juice or prune juice.

Date Juice: This is incredibly sweet, so use as a sweetener instead of sugar. Goes very well with fresh apple or pear juice, sour orange juice or grapefruit juice.

11.

JAMS, CHUTNEYS, PICKLES AND SAUCES

DRIED APRICOT JAM

Dried apricots have very little setting properties so you will need to use commercial pectin. Buy a liquid kind and follow instructions on the pack regarding the amount to use.

Imperial (Metric)	American
½ lb (225g) dried apricots	1½ cupsful dried apricots
Water	Water
3 lb (1.3 kilos) raw cane sugar	8 cupsful raw cane sugar
Juice of a lemon	Juice of a lemon
Commercial pectin	Commercial pectin

1. Soak the apricots in water overnight.

2. The next day simmer in a saucepan with the lid on for about 30 minutes. This should give you about 1½ lb/680g (3¾ cupsful) but if it has worked out to less, top up with more water.

3. Add the lemon juice and sugar. Bring to the boil for 1 minute.

4. Take off the heat and stir in the correct amount of liquid pectin.

5. Put into hot jars and seal.

Note: Depending on the apricots you may need to skim the hot jam before potting.

SWEET MINCEMEAT

This is a recipe where dried fruit really comes into its own. Although early versions of this traditional pie filling contained real meat it has now become a mixture of fruit and spices. Commercial types of mincemeat still contain meat — in the form of beef suet — but this recipe uses margarine instead.

Imperial (Metric)	American
3 oz (85g) sultanas	½ cupful golden seedless raisins
2 oz (55g) seedless raisins	⅓ cupful seedless raisins
3 oz (85g) currants	½ cupful currants
2 oz (55g) raw cane sugar	⅓ cupful raw cane sugar
1 medium apple, finely grated	1 medium apple, finely grated
2 oz (55g) chopped almonds	⅓ cupful chopped almonds
½ teaspoonful allspice	½ teaspoonful allspice
½ teaspoonful cinnamon	½ teaspoonful cinnamon
½ teaspoonful freshly grated nutmeg	½ teaspoonful freshly grated nutmeg
Grated rind of 1 lemon	Grated rind of 1 lemon
2 oz (55g) melted margarine	5 tablespoonsful melted margarine
1 tablespoonful brandy	1 tablespoonful brandy
Orange juice	Orange juice

1. Blend all ingredients except the orange juice, in a bowl. Mix well.

2. Moisten with orange juice — about 1 tablespoonful should be sufficient.

3. Put into jars, cover and store in the fridge until required.

Note: This will keep for several weeks in the fridge. Used traditionally for mince pies and tarts at Christmas but can be used all the year round too. Once you have eaten home-made mincemeat the commercially-made varieties pale into insignificance.

PLUM MINCEMEAT

This is another variation of sweet mincemeat with a base of fresh plums and quite different spices from Sweet Mincemeat. This recipe will keep for several months.

Imperial (Metric)	American
2 lb (900g) fresh plums	2 pounds fresh plums
Grated rind of 1 lemon	Grated rind of 1 lemon
5 tablespoonsful water	¼ cupful water
4 large cooking apples	4 large cooking apples
2 oz (55g) currants	⅓ cupful currants
2 oz (55g) raisins	⅓ cupful raisins
2 oz (55g) sultanas	⅓ cupful golden seedless raisins
Grated rind of 1 orange	Grated rind of 1 orange
2 oz (55g) chopped almonds	½ cupful chopped almonds
1 teaspoonful ground ginger	1 teaspoonful ground ginger
1 teaspoonful cinnamon	1 teaspoonful cinnamon
1 teaspoonful ground cloves	1 teaspoonful ground cloves
½ lb (225g) raw cane sugar	1 cupful raw cane sugar
Juice of ½ a lemon	Juice of ½ a lemon

1. Wash plums and remove stones.

2. Put into a pan with the lemon juice and water. Simmer until cooked and soft.

3. Allow to cool and blend in a liquidizer.

4. Mix with all other ingredients.

5. Spoon into clean jars, cover and seal.

Note: Use for pies and tarts. An unusual form of mincemeat, fruity and spicy.

APRICOT & LEMON MARMALADE

Imperial (Metric)	American
1 lb (455g) lemons	1 pound lemons
1 lb (455g) dried apricots, cut into pieces	1 pound dried apricots, cut into pieces

3 pints (1.7 litres) water	7½ cupsful water
3 lb (1.3 kilos) soft moist cane sugar	3 pounds soft moist cane sugar

1. Cut the lemons in half. Squeeze out the juice and put all the pips to one side. Cut the skins into small pieces, or, put through a mincer.

2. Tie the pips in a piece of muslin.

3. Soak all the fruit overnight in the water.

4. The following day heat and simmer until the fruit has softened, with the muslin bag of pips. Remove this and discard.

5. Add the lemon juice, then the sugar. Stir while you heat until all the sugar has dissolved.

6. Boil rapidly until it sets.

7. Pour into clean jars, cover with waxed circles and tie on covers.

8. Date and label the jars.

Note: Makes a very dark kind of breakfast marmalade that can be made all the year round, especially when lemons are cheap.

DRIED FRUIT CHUTNEY

Warning: Iron or copper pans are not suitable for making chutneys etc., which contain vinegar. Use stainless steel or aluminium ones.

Imperial (Metric)	American
1 lb (455g) dried apricots	1 pound dried apricots
4 oz (115g) stoned prunes	¾ cupful stoned prunes
½ lb (225g) sultanas	1½ cupsful golden seedless raisins
½ lb (225g) raisins	1½ cupsful raisins
4 cloves garlic, peeled	4 cloves garlic, peeled
Grated rind and juice of 1 lemon	Grated rind and juice of 1 lemon
Grated rind and juice of 1 orange	Grated rind and juice of 1 orange
2 pints (1.1 litres) wine vinegar	5 cupsful wine vinegar
2 tablespoonsful pickling spices	2 tablepoonsful pickling spices
2 lb (900g) raw cane sugar	2 pounds raw cane sugar
2½ lb (1.25 kilos) cooking apples	2½ pounds cooking apples

1. Cut the apricots and prunes into small pieces.

2. Soak for a couple of hours in water, so that the fruit softens.

3. Drain well and put into a large pan.

4. Add the remaining dried fruit. Crush in the garlic and add the fruit juices and rinds. Stir well.

5. Pour in about a quarter of the vinegar with the pickling spices, tied in a muslin bag.

6. Bring to the boil and cook steadily for about 30 minutes, adding the rest of the vinegar.

7. Put in the sugar and apples (peeled and coarsely grated).

8. Bring to the boil again and cook steadily for another 15 to 20 minutes until thick. Stir from time to time.

9. Take out the pickling spices and discard.

10. Pour chutney into hot jars, cover with waxed paper and seal tightly. Label with the name and date.

11. Store in a cool, dry place — preferably in the dark.

TOMATO CHUTNEY

Imperial (Metric)	American
½ teaspoonful pickling spice	½ teaspoonful pickling spice
2 oz (55g) chopped (peeled) onion	⅓ cupful chopped (peeled) onion
3 tablespoonsful wine vinegar	4 tablespoonsful wine vinegar
1 cooking apple, peeled and chopped	1 cooking apple, peeled and chopped
½ lb (225g) fresh tomatoes, sliced	2 cupsful fresh sliced tomatoes
3 pinches ground ginger	3 pinches ground ginger
½ level teaspoonful dry mustard	½ level teaspoonful dry mustard
3 grinds freshly ground black pepper	3 grinds freshly ground black pepper
3 pinches sea salt	3 pinches sea salt
2 oz (55g) sultanas	⅓ cupful golden seedless raisins
2 oz (55g) raw cane sugar	⅓ cupful raw cane sugar

1. Tie the pickling spices in a piece of muslin.

2. Put the chopped onion into a saucepan with the vinegar and simmer until the onion has softened.

3. Put in the chopped apple, tomato slices, ginger, mustard, seasoning and dried fruit.

4. Bring to the boil and simmer until soft, giving the mixture a stir from time to time.

5. Sprinkle in the sugar and boil steadily until the mixture looks like jam.

6. Take out the pickling spice bag and discard.

7. Pour into a clean, warm jar, cover with a waxed disc and seal immediately.

8. Serve with cheese and biscuits, in sandwiches or with curry.

AUTUMN CHUTNEY

Imperial (Metric)
1 lb (455g) stoned plums
1 lb (455g) apples, peeled, cored
  and chopped
1 lb (455g) tomatoes, chopped
1 lb (455g) onion, peeled and
  chopped
1 clove garlic, peeled
¼ teaspoonful each of ground mace,
  mixed spice and cayenne pepper
½ pint (285ml) cider vinegar
3 teaspoonsful ground ginger
½ lb (225g) sultanas
½ lb (225g) raw cane sugar

American
1 pound stoned plums
2½ cupsful chopped apple
2½ cupsful chopped tomatoes
1 pound onions, peeled and chopped
1 clove garlic, peeled
¼ teaspoonful each of ground mace,
  mixed spice and cayenne pepper
1⅓ cupsful cider vinegar
3 teaspoonsful ground ginger
1½ cupsful golden seedless raisins
1⅓ cupsful raw cane sugar

1. Put all the prepared vegetables and fruit into a large pan and sprinkle with the spices.

2. Pour in the vinegar and bring to the boil.

3. Cook until everything is tender then add the sugar.

4. Cook until thick, stirring from time to time.

5. Put into hot jars, cover and seal.

APRICOT CHUTNEY

Imperial (Metric)
1 lb (455g) dried apricots
1 lb (455g) onions, peeled and
  sliced
1½ pints (850ml) cider vinegar
Juice and peel of 1 lemon
Juice and peel of 1 orange
5 oz (140g) raisins, chopped
5 oz (140g) sultanas
1 lb (455g) raw cane sugar
1 tablespoonful pickling spice in a
  muslin bag
½ teaspoonful cinnamon

American
2½ cupsful dried apricots
2½ cupsful sliced onions
3¾ cupsful cider vinegar
Juice and peel of 1 lemon
Juice and peel of 1 orange
1 cupful raisins, chopped
1 cupful golden seedless raisins
2½ cupsful raw cane sugar
1 tablespoonful pickling spice in a
  muslin bag
½ teaspoonful cinnamon

1. Soak the apricots overnight. Drain and chop coarsely.

2. Put the onions into a large saucepan with a little of the vinegar. Bring to the boil and simmer for 5 minutes.

3. Add all other ingredients except sugar. Boil steadily for 30 minutes or simmer gently for about 2 hours until the chutney has thickened.

4. Take out and discard pickling spices.

5. Put chutney into hot jars. Cover and seal.

6. Store in a cool dry place. Use as required.

Note: Use with curries, bread and cheese and in sandwiches.

QUICK APPLE CHUTNEY

1 cooking apple, peeled and cored
1 small onion, peeled and chopped
1 heaped tablespoonful raw cane sugar
4 pinches ground ginger
Sprinkle of sultanas (golden seedless raisins) or chopped, stoned dates
3 tablespoonsful wine or cider vinegar

1. Grate the apple and put into a small saucepan with the chopped onion.

2. Cook while you stir for about 10 minutes.

3. Put into a jar and eat within a week.

Note: If you rarely use chutney and it is not worth your while to make a large amount, use this recipe to make just a small pot. Use it up within 3 or 4 days as it will not keep like other chutneys.

PICKLED PRUNES

For people (like me) who hate black olives and love pizza, these pickled prunes can make a good substitute. Chop into olive-sized pieces. Also use for decoration on open sandwiches or with bread and cheese.

Imperial (Metric)	American
4 oz (115g) stoned prunes	2/3 cupful stoned prunes
1/4 pint (140ml) wine vinegar	2/3 cupful wine vinegar
6 tablespoonsful water	6 tablespoonsful water
1/2 teaspoonful cinnamon	1/2 teaspoonful cinnamon
4 oz (115g) raw cane sugar	2/3 cupful raw cane sugar

1. Put the prunes into a basin and pour in the vinegar and water.

2. Sprinkle with the cinnamon and sugar. Leave to soak overnight.

3. The next day transfer to a saucepan and bring to the boil. Simmer for about 15 minutes.

4. Cool and strain, reserving juice.

5. Pack into a storage jar. Bring the juice to the boil and then pour into the jar.

6. Leave to grow cold then cover.

7. Use as required, replacing the cover each time.

Note: The fruit is best left for 6 to 8 weeks before opening.

SPICED DRIED FRUITS

Serve instead of chutney.

Imperial (Metric)	American
1 pint (570ml) wine vinegar	2 1/2 cupsful wine vinegar
1 level tablespoonful pickling spice	1 tablespoonful pickling spice
1 lb (455g) dried fruit salad	3 cupsful dried fruit salad
4 oz (115g) raw cane sugar	2/3 cupful raw cane sugar

1. Put the pickling spice into a saucepan with the vinegar and boil for about 15 minutes.

2. Strain and discard the spices.

3. Pour the vinegar over the dried fruit and leave overnight.

4. The next day, add the sugar and bring to the boil.

5. Simmer until all the fruit is soft but still unbroken.

6. Pack into jars and seal.

BROWN FRUIT SAUCE

Scrupulously clean and scalded commercial sauce bottles are ideal for bottling this sauce.

Imperial (Metric)	American
6 oz (170g) stoned dates, chopped	1 cupful stoned dates, chopped
4 medium fresh tomatoes, chopped	4 medium fresh tomatoes, chopped
1 large cooking apple, peeled and chopped	1 large cooking apple, peeled and chopped
4 oz (115g) onion, peeled and chopped	2/3 cupful onion, peeled and chopped
Scant 1/4 pint (140ml) wine vinegar	1/2 cupful wine vinegar
2 tablespoonsful fresh lemon juice	2 tablespoonsful fresh lemon juice
1/3 pint (200ml) water	Scant cupful water
1 clove garlic, peeled	1 clove garlic, peeled
4 teaspoonsful thin soya sauce	4 teaspoonsful thin soy sauce
1/2 teaspoonful ground ginger	1/2 teaspoonful ground ginger
4 pinches ground cloves	4 pinches ground cloves
1/2 teaspoonful sea salt	1/2 teaspoonful sea salt
1 tablespoonful raw cane sugar	1 tablespoonful raw cane sugar

1. Put the dates, tomatoes, apple and onion into an aluminium or steel pan with the vinegar. Cook until soft.

2. Remove from heat and add the lemon juice and water.

3. Put into liquidizer and blend to a smooth sauce.

4. Pour back into pan and crush in the garlic, add the soya sauce, spices, salt and sugar.

5. Stir while you heat to reduce the sauce.

6. Put through a fine mesh sieve to remove pips.

7. Pour into clean jars, or, through a funnel into sauce bottles.

8. Allow to grow cold and then cover, or, screw on lids.

9. Store in the fridge.

12.

DRIED FRUIT IN SPECIAL DIETS

Every now and then you may have to cater for someone on a special diet as well as the rest of the family. This idea can throw the most expert cook into a panic. Very often, people on special diets who have not made any special effort to come to terms with a new eating regime, or who are new to the situation, wrongly believe that a special diet has to be boring. This is not helped by a panicky hostess or a well-meaning cook who makes a great deal of fuss and extra work for herself.

You will find some recipes in this book suitable for particular diets anyway. These are indicated in this section.

There is not room in this book for many special diet recipes using dried fruit but I have included a few guidelines and basic recipes to put dried fruit into this context and a little nutritional information that may prove helpful.

If you can, as a matter of courtesy, check the list of ingredients that you plan to use for a special recipe with the special dieter or the person who caters for them. This can save disappointment and wasted effort.

Of all the people on special diets I find difficult to cater for, the drastic slimmer is the one I dread most. Most of them will just pick at whatever you have prepared and look enviously at everyone else tucking in. However, the situation has improved since high-fibre low-fat/low-sugar diets have become popular. Here are two pudding recipes (always the most difficult of courses for the slimmer) which are high in fibre, very low in fat and sugar. In spite of this they still look and taste like substantial puddings and will be greeted with enthusiasm by the rest of the non-dieting family.

(Food value tables prepared from McCance and Widdowson.)

Fibre Value Chart — approx. fibre content per edible portion

Dried fruit:	g of fibre
figs (raw)	19
figs (stewed)	10
peaches and pears (raw)	14
peaches and pears (stewed)	5
Dates (pitted)	9
sultanas and stoned raisins	7
apricots (raw)	24
apricots (stewed)	9
prunes (raw)	16
prunes (stewed without stones)	8
currants	4

Extra High-fibre, Low-fat, Low-sugar

BROWN BETTY
Serves 3 to 4

Imperial (Metric)
4 oz (115g) dried fruit (see note)
3 oz (85g) rolled oats
½ oz (7g) wheatgerm
½ oz (7g) bran
Finely grated rind of 1 small lemon
Juice of 1 small lemon
½ lb (225g) cooking apples, cored and sliced thinly
Raw cane sugar to taste

American
⅔ cupful dried fruit (see note)
⅔ cupful rolled oats
1 slightly heaped tablespoonful wheatgerm
1 slightly heaped tablespoonful bran
Finely grated rind of 1 small lemon
Juice of 1 small lemon
½ pound cooking apples, cored and sliced thinly
Raw cane sugar to taste

1. Soak the dried fruit overnight in cold water. The next day, cook for about 15 minutes in more water. Reserve the juice.

2. Preheat the oven at 350°F/180°C (Gas Mark 4).

3. Melt the margarine in a saucepan and stir in the oats, wheatgerm, bran and rind. Mix well to absorb the margarine.

4. Put the lemon juice into an ovenproof dish with 3 tablespoonsful of the dried fruit juice.

5. Cover the base of the dish with half the apple slices. Sprinkle with a little raw cane sugar and cover with ¼ of the oat mixture.

6. Chop the dried fruit and use ½ to cover the layer of oat mixture.

7. Continue until you have 4 layers of fruit and 4 of the oat mixture, finishing with the latter on top.

8. Bake above centre of oven for about 30 minutes or until browned.

9. Serve for pudding, hot, with reheated dried fruit juice as a sauce. (The rest of the family who are not dieting may like it with real custard.)

Note: For the dried fruit — use pears, peaches or apricots.

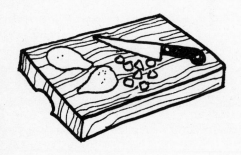

BAKED FRUITY APPLES

Use the instructions for Baked Stuffed Apples on page 43 but for the stuffing use a mixture of chopped, stoned prunes, dried apricots and raisins. Mix with a scrape of polyunsaturated margarine and a little orange juice. Use generously to stuff the cored apples. Very high in fibre.

Low Sodium (Salt)

On a strict low-sodium diet dried fruits (except dates) are not allowed as they contain too much sodium.

Sodium Value Chart — approx. sodium content per 100g edible portion

Dried fruit:	*mg of sodium*
apples	5
dates (pitted)	5
pears	7
prunes	8
currants	9
seedless raisins	16
peaches	16
stoned raisins	52
sultanas (golden seedless raisins)	52
figs	87

Special baking powder must be used in low-sodium cooking as ordinary baking powders and self-raising flours are not low in sodium. Only butter or margarine labelled 'low-sodium', 'salt-free' or 'unsalted' should be used.

The recipe for Date Slices on page 96 is suitable if unsalted butter or margarine is used. (Ignore the fruit variation at the foot of the recipe as this does not apply to low-sodium diets.)

The recipe for Date Twists on page 93 can be used if unsalted butter or margarine is used. The nuts must also be unsalted.

A simple low-sodium sweet: Slices of orange sprinkled with chopped dates and a little raw cane sugar. Allow at least 1 orange and 1 date per person. Serve in glass dishes.

Extra Iron

Poor eating habits or ill-health that can lead to anaemia may not mean the diet is just too low in iron but other components such as Vitamin B_{12}, Vitamin C and protein. Dried fruits can be useful as a source of iron, especially if taken regularly in the form of juices. Dried apricot or peach juice would seem to be the most beneficial, having the highest content of iron.

Iron Value Chart — approx. iron content per 100g edible protein.

Dried fruit:	mg of iron
apricots	6
peaches	6
prunes	4
figs	4
currants	3
sultanas (golden seedless raisins)	2
stoned raisins	2
seedless raisins	2
pears	1

Compote (page 50), Dried Fruit Salad (page 47), Fruit Salad Pie (page 80) and Apricot Plate Pie (page 82). Plain stewed dried fruit such as apricots, peaches, prunes and figs all have a high iron content.

Allergies

The most common allergies are to staple foods such as wheat, milk and eggs. Allergies to dried fruits are comparatively rare unless the person is allergic to fresh fruits.

Here is the recipe for an unusual fruit cake for allergics. It took me years of experimenting to arrive at this version which looks and tastes like an ordinary wholefood fruit cake. (Something like this is so welcome to an allergic who may be very restricted in just what he or she can eat.)

FRUIT CAKE

For those allergic to one or more of the following: wheat, corn, gluten, rye, barley, oats, eggs, milk, cane and beet sugar.

Imperial (Metric)	American
¼ pint (140ml) fresh orange juice	⅔ cupful fresh orange juice
2 tablespoonsful fructose (fruit sugar)	2 tablespoonsful fructose (fruit sugar)
¼ oz (7g) active dried yeast	½ tablespoonful active dried yeast
3 tablespoonsful vegetable oil	3 tablespoonsful vegetable oil
1 oz (30g) soya flour	¼ cupful soy flour
5 oz (140g) ground brown rice	⅔ cupful ground brown rice
2 oz (55g) ground almonds	½ cupful ground almonds
1 eating apple, washed and cut into pieces	1 eating apple, washed and cut into pieces
1½ oz (45g) fresh carrot, scrubbed and grated	2 heaped tablespoonsful grated carrot
½ lb (225g) dried fruit (currants, sultanas, raisins, chopped dried apricots)	1½ cupsful dried fruit (currants, golden seedless raisins, raisins, chopped dried apricots)
Grated rind of 1 lemon or 1 orange	Grated rind of 1 lemon or 1 orange

1. Preheat oven at 350°F/180°C (Gas Mark 4).

2. Warm the fruit juice and pour into the liquidizer goblet.

3. Sprinkle in the dried yeast and leave to soften for a few minutes with the sugar.

4. Put the oil into a mixing bowl and add the soya flour, ground rice and almonds.

5. Add the pieces of apple and grated carrot to the mixture in the liquidizer and blend. Pour over the flour mix.

6. Stir well and add the dried fruit of your choice. Mix again to a very sloppy consistency.

7. Oil a 7 in. (18cm) round cake tin. Spoon the mixture into this and flatten the top with a knife.

8. Bake on the top shelf for about an hour.

9. Cool in the tin for about 30 minutes then turn out carefully on to a wire rack to finish cooling.

10. Store in an airtight container and eat within 7 days.

Note: This may seem a combination of extraordinary ingredients but it produces a rich, moist fruit cake. 1 heaped teaspoonful of cinnamon can be added if desired and the top can be decorated with almonds before baking to make it more attractive. Don't be afraid to hand this cake round — no one will ever know the difference.

If there is no allergy to cane or beet sugar then use raw cane sugar instead of fructose. If there is an allergy to almonds use another kind of nut such as cashews or walnuts. Apart from this small amount of tinkering, please proceed as per recipe for best results.

FRUIT COOKIES
Makes 5. Free of wheat, gluten, rye, barley, oats, corn and egg.

Imperial (Metric)	**American**
1 oz (30g) polyunsaturated margarine	2½ tablespoonsful polyunsaturated margarine
2 oz (55g) brown ground rice	¼ cupful ground brown rice
1 oz (30g) raw cane sugar	1 heaped tablespoonful raw cane sugar
1½ oz (45g) finely grated eating apple	2 heaped tablespoonsful finely grated eating apple
Finely grated rind of ½ an orange	Finely grated rind of ½ an orange
½ oz (15g) currants, raisins or sultanas	2 tablespoonsful currants, raisins or golden seedless raisins

1. Preheat oven at 450°F/230°C (Gas Mark 8).

2. Put the margarine into a bowl with the ground rice and blend with a fork. Add all remaining ingredients and knead into 1 ball of dough.

3. Grease a baking sheet and spoon the dough onto it in 5 heaps, leaving plenty of space around each one.

4. Spread into cookie shapes with a knife.

5. Bake for about 20 to 25 minutes, until browned.

6. Allow to cool on the baking sheet and then remove with a spatula and put on to a wire rack to cool.

7. Eat warm or on the same day of baking.

Note: This recipe can also be made milk-free by using a milk-free margarine (one that does not contain milk solids or whey). Use both for the cookies and for greasing the baking sheet.

Variation: ¼ teaspoonful cinnamon can be added for variation. The orange rind can be omitted if the spice is used instead.

A useful recipe for coeliacs who cannot tolerate gluten, and for wheat and corn allergics as well as those who cannot tolerate eggs.

Low-Fat
All dried fruits are extremely low in fat. Plain soaked and cooked apricots, peaches, prunes or pears with a little sugar make an excellent sweet. See recipes for Dried Fruit Salad (page 47) and Dried Fruit Compote (page 50).

Extra Calcium

The most important factor in the diet for healthy teeth and bones is calcium. Most of us get our supply from milk, cheese and bread. However, dried fruit can be used to top up the amount of calcium we are taking, bearing in mind the dried fruits which give you the highest amounts.

Calcium Value Chart — approx. calcium per 100g edible portion.

Dried fruit:	mg of calcium
figs	280
currants	88
apricots	67
dates	65
stoned raisins	61
seedless raisins	54
sultanas (golden seedless raisins)	52
prunes (stoned)	51
peaches	48
pears	35
apples	31

High-Potassium

Since some of us take as much as 30 times too much salt and as little as a quarter of the potassium we need to keep the sodium/potassium balance in our bodies it is worth considering dried fruit in this context. (The best source of potassium in the diet could be fresh vegetables but few people eat large enough amounts or cook them to avoid potassium loss.) For maximum potassium value eat raw pears, prunes and dates. If reconstituting, also use the soaked juices for blending or as a juice.

High-Potassium/Low-Sodium Value Chart — approx. potassium/sodium per 100g portion

Dried fruit:	mg potassium	mg sodium
apples	569	5
pears	573	7
prunes	694	8
dates (stoned)	750	5
currants	747	9

Low-Calorie

Dried fruits are high in natural sugars so are not really in the low-calorie league. However, 2 oz (55g) dried figs or prunes, cooked without sugar will make a satisfying sweet, breakfast fruit or snack at less than 110 calories.

All the recipes in this book are designed for a healthy diet. Food should not be merely an entertainment for the palate and eye and nothing more. (This doesn't mean to say healthy food cannot also look and taste appetizing.) People who are not in need tend to overdo their food and live as if everyday is a festival. Breaking all the rules once in a while won't be harmful in the long run, but breaking them everyday can be health suicide. (See the section on nutrition for the rules — page 8.)

Any good bookshop or health store should have a selection of literature and books on healthier eating. As the level of education on nutrition is usually abysmal for most of us, start educating yourself through reading, at your own pace. The knowledge is there for everyone — it just needs a little time and application.

INDEX